The Huddled Masses: Immigration and Inequality

Katy Long

CONTENTS

ACKNOWLEDGMENTS

This book could not have been completed without the help of many people, who over the past two years have contributed their thoughts, critiques and experiences and have undoubtedly made *The Huddled Masses* a better book in the process. Though I've begged favours from too many people to thank them all here individually, particular thanks is due to Sam Vincent for reading an early draft of the book proposal, to Laura-Jane Smith for her help with some very early chapters, and to Jennifer Allsopp, Sarah Clarke and Sarah-Jane Cooper-Knock for reading the draft manuscript. Above all, thanks is due to Tim Moreton for giving me the confidence to pursue a very different sort of writing project.

I was also very lucky to benefit from having the time to carry out the research for *The Huddled Masses* while working at the London School of Economics and the University of Edinburgh, and while spending time as a Visiting Scholar at Stanford University. I am also very grateful to Andrew Lownie for agreeing to take on this project at an early stage and who, as my agent, has helped to shape it into the finished product. Thanks too to Chris Fagg for copyediting the manuscript, and Andrew Rosenheim at Amazon for adding the final touches for adding the final touches to the Kindle Single version of the work. *The Huddled Masses* could not have been written without their help, but of course any errors and omissions are mine alone.

1 THE FEAR FACTOR

Too often we enjoy the comfort of opinion without the discomfort of thought.

John F. Kennedy, Yale Commencement Address, 11 July 1962

Be afraid: the immigrants are coming. From warnings of Romanians rushing across the channel into the UK, to Mexican traffickers breaching America's borders, we are repeatedly told that a flood of new arrivals threatens to swamp our cultures, our communities and our livelihoods.

Worse: we are told that immigration threatens to undo the gains of a century of progressive politics, exacerbating a rising tide of inequality, as – in the words of UK Home Secretary Theresa May – 'uncontrolled, mass immigration displaces British workers, forces people onto benefits, and suppresses wages for the low-paid'.[1]

This book is about the actual, rather than the perceived relationship between immigration and inequality. Inequality has been called – in the words of US president Barack Obama – 'the defining challenge of our time'.[2] Inequality is growing. One percent of the world's population owns more than half of the world's wealth. In the US, the wealthiest 1% has captured more than 95% of post-2009 economic growth. In the UK, five wealthy families own more than the poorest 20% of the British population.[3] Economists such as Thomas Piketty warn of the pitfalls of rising income inequality and the ills that follow.[4] In part because of these worries, in the past decade immigration has become a politically toxic topic, with prophecies of doom dominating election campaigns and filling tabloid headlines.

In this version of immigration's ills, 'a wealthy metropolitan elite' may benefit from Polish plumbers and Bulgarian nannies, but the 'ordinary, hard-working people of this country' do not: instead, they lose wages, jobs and opportunities that were previously theirs.[5] Capital grows richer: native workers grow poorer. As a result, 'progressive' politicians and analysts such as David Goodhart, author of *The British Dream*, claim that working to reduce inequality at home demands stricter restrictions be placed on immigration, which has 'exacerbated many of the undesirable aspects of British economic life: poverty, inequality, low productivity...'. [6] It's a seductive narrative: the success of the anti-immigration United Kingdom Independence Party (UKIP) in the May 2014 European elections was partly a result of a campaign that insisted immigrants keep Britons poor.[7]

This short book argues the opposite. There is in fact overwhelming evidence that enabling freedom of movement can play a vital role in combating poverty and opening up opportunity, not just for immigrants and shorter-term foreign workers, but for the poor here too. The problem isn't migration as much as the immigration *system*. In recent years Western governments have increasingly chosen to restrict the rights of the poor to move – and this is fast turning legal migration into a privilege accessible only to corporations or those with personal wealth. This is regressive politics. It's *these* immigration policies that entrench inequality – at both a national *and* a global scale, by rendering the poor immobile in both geographic and economic terms. This book shows not only *how* our migration policies are hindering rather than helping the fight for social mobility, but also suggests ways we might begin to reverse the trend.

One difficulty in talking about immigration and inequality is that migration policies increasingly rely not on research and reason but anecdote and sentiment. Instead of evidence, we have emotions: UK Home Secretary Theresa May promising to create a 'hostile environment' for undocumented migrants and waving the *Daily Mail* at the despatch box in Westminster.[8] The news in 2013 that 'up to 29 million' Romanians and Bulgarians would come to the UK to claim benefits once restrictions on freedom of movement were lifted (which, if true, would have required the entire population of both countries to emigrate) is a good example of how inaccurate reporting and distorted figures feed what the International Organisation for Migration has called 'the biased, polarized and negative debate' on migration, not just in the UK 'but around the world'.[9]

Given these distortions, how can we start to investigate the real relationships between immigration and inequality? One good place to begin is with the recognition that most people in the UK think immigration *is* a serious problem, and believe that there should be far less of it. Just under a fifth of British voters say that migration is *the* most important political issue facing the UK today: over a quarter agree that immigration is 'very likely' to affect the way they vote at the next General Election.[10] The importance attached by voters to the issue of migration explains why the issue is so salient for politicians. In the UK, Labour leader Ed Miliband has been forced to apologise for Labour's past immigration policies.[11] Prime Minister and Tory leader David Cameron has repeatedly asserted that 'immigration [is] far too high and badly out of control'.[12]

Many anti-immigration groups – including UKIP – use the language of crisis, presenting contemporary immigration in overwhelming terms. Goodhart, for instance, warns us that 'more people [now] arrive on these shores as immigrants *in a single year* than in the entire period 1066 to 1950'.[13] Yet considered in proportional terms, the story looks more complex. When 50,000 Huguenots refugees arrived from France in the late 1680s the total population of England and Wales was only 5 million. The equivalent today would be half a million Syrian Christians arriving to seek sanctuary – not the 500 the UK government agreed to admit in early 2014, nor the 50 it had admitted by July 2014.[14]

The long view also shows us that neither migration nor our fears about migration are so new or unusual. Immigration control has been a point of contention for centuries: we have usually tended to think our cities and states are full up, and admitted newcomers with bad grace. Blanket immigration controls have often been imposed in populist haste, and repented at leisure. No one needs to be told now that restricting Jewish immigration in the 1930s came at a terrible human cost; but it's worth remembering that in 1938 *The Daily Mail* was still warning the British public about the dangerous German Jews 'pouring' into the country.[15] From the 1882 US Chinese Exclusion Act that locked out all Chinese labourers from the United States, through the White Australia immigration policies that were only finally dismantled in 1973, every great wave of migration has been followed by popular outcry and legislative restrictions intended to prevent the poor from moving. The UK first legislated to restrict (primarily Jewish) immigration from Eastern Europe in 1905 – because of fears that Britain was becoming 'the sink of the most undesirable class of aliens on the Continent'.[16]

This is not the whole story. In imploring the Old World to 'Give me your tired, your poor ... Your huddled masses yearning to breathe free, The wretched refuse of your teeming shore', the inscription at the base of the Statue of Liberty in New York Harbour is a century-old testament to our recognition that migration also has the power to offer an escape from misery and poverty.[17] But if the liberation that migration can bring has long been recognised, the effects of allowing the poor to move across borders have been equally long feared.

And it's not just a question of history: there is also present-day paradox in our attitudes towards immigration. Despite widespread hostility, modern capitalist societies clearly depend upon immigrants. In fact, academics have long puzzled over this 'policy gap', seeking to understand why, despite the rhetoric, governments accept unwanted immigration.[18] The answer? It's the economy, stupid. Businesses profit from high-skilled migrants' in-demand talents, as well as the willingness of many other migrants – especially those without documents or legal status – to work long hours for poor pay. Universities depend upon foreign students' fees. In other words, migration plays a fundamental role in greasing the wheels of capitalist growth. Given increasing concern about how capitalist economics may lead inexorably to widening inequality, this suggests that if we really want to reduce inequality and poverty, immigration policies may well need to change.

But it's not clear that change necessarily means less migration. It may just mean *different* migration. Designing immigration policy isn't just a quantitative but a qualitative task: we need to ask not just *how much* but also *what sort* of migration is best suited to combating poverty and inequality. We need to ask *in whose interest* existing migration policies have been designed. Do bars on low-skilled migration really protect the poor – either here or there?

Of course, you can't only talk about immigration in abstract, technical terms: behind every migration is an intensely personal story. My own migration history, for instance, is a reminder that migration is not just a one-way journey, but is often circular and temporary. I was born in the northeast of England, and I grew up between England and Canada, emigrating – and returning – twice before I settled in Kent, aged 12. I have two passports: I'm not sure I have a hometown. In an unexpected twist, while writing this book I found myself preparing for a third emigration, this time to the United States. I wrote the final words of this book in San Francisco, arguably the quintessential twenty-first century migrants' city.

So I know migration from the inside: measuring excitement, adventure and freedom against loneliness, dislocation and exhaustion. But I also know migration from the outside. It's an irony that many public figures who argue that we need to move quickly to restrict migration are often quick to point to their own family history as the sons and spouses of immigrants, seemingly untroubled by reconciling their own present-day elite cosmopolitan freedoms with protectionist views on migration for the masses.[19] In my case, aside from the odd Scot or Ulsterman, my recent ancestors appear to have been a remarkably unadventurous bunch. I am indisputably part of Britain's white, English majority. I've spent the vast majority of my adult life living in southeast England, a local in a landscape that's as close to John Major's English Arcadia as you are likely to find. I have been a 'local' far longer than I've been an 'immigrant'.

My migration story is nevertheless one shaped by social mobility and privilege. I've travelled freely across five continents. Our emigration to the US was smoothed by corporate money. My personal experience and understanding of migration – both as a local and as a newcomer – is clearly likely to be vastly different from that of a manual worker with few qualifications. But I believe that with that privilege comes responsibility. Here, the responsibility is to acknowledge that – despite the EU's supposed commitment to freedom of movement for EU citizen workers – migration is actually increasingly inaccessible to the average citizen. This means that the poor over there are not only 'kept out', *but that they are also locked in here*. As this book will show, this is a problem if we care about building a more equal, progressive society.

This connection between the *de facto* restrictions on migration and poverty is amplified once we think in global rather than national terms. We rarely have to confront the enormity of global inequality. But this book is partly motivated by the sense of burning shame I felt standing outside a one-room shack in a Kampala slum – home to a young Congolese man, a refugee and a university graduate – as he asked me why I was allowed to visit him in Uganda, but he could not come to see me in the UK.

What follows is an attempt to atone for the inadequacy of my answer then. It is also an attempt to show those who advocate further restrictions on migration in the name of progressive politics that our entire migration system is increasingly an instrument of regression, entrenching inequality and diminishing the freedoms of the poor – including 'our' poor at home that these rules and regulations are ostensibly designed to protect.

The Huddled Masses starts by looking at the language we use to talk about immigration, and the statistics that offer us a snapshot of what international migration really looks like – and how this differs from tabloid concerns. Having established this empirical baseline, the book moves on to consider first principles. Is global justice or national solidarity more important? Should we start with borders, or freedom of movement? It then considers the issue of where we should draw the borders that decide who's in and who's out. Is EU freedom of movement a bold experiment in the name of progressive politics, or illiberal fortress-building?

In Chapter 5, I follow the money, looking at who gains from policing – or piercing – a legal migration system that only the wealthy can access. I then look at the ways in which not only migration but citizenship is increasingly offered for sale – and consider what this means for equality. I also look at whether our existing refugee and asylum systems offer an adequate safety net for those who flee in fear of their lives, but can't pay the market price for migration.

The final third of the book comes closer to home, investigating whether migration really has any effect on local unemployment and wages – and concluding that the effects are minimal, and that in some circumstances it's actually strict migration controls that are exacerbating the problem.

It's clear from the evidence that immigration and inequality *are* inextricably linked. But it's equally clear that this link is often misunderstood and distorted in the calculation of private political interest. In the name of 'protecting' the poor, the West is in fact building migration systems that are explicitly set up to make it harder for them to move at all, while facilitating the easy mobility of the rich. The result is an immigration system that is entrenching inequality – both abroad and here at home. In the final chapter, I suggest how we might begin to change this, so that immigration policies support social mobility, and discussion about migration is no longer dominated by fear, but by facts.

2 THE THREE PERCENT

Migrant: Brit. / ˈmʌɪɡr(ə)nt/ , *U.S.* / ˈmaɪɡr(ə)nt/
   1.   A person who moves temporarily or seasonally from place to place; †a person on a journey
   2.   A person who moves permanently to live in a new country, town, etc., esp. to look for work, or to take up a post, etc.; an immigrant.
   Oxford English Dictionary

Who is a migrant? When angry voters complain about how 'immigration is ruining this country', migrants melt into a single amorphous mass, identified by a single common factor of being *here*, but coming from *there*. Yet migrants' experiences are infinitely varied, shaped by factors including education, ethnicity, wealth – and luck. In this chapter, we'll investigate the gap between our perceptions of 'migrants' and the reality of migration – and consider what this says about our prejudices.

As soon as you begin asking the question 'who is a migrant?' the gap between what we *think* we know and what is actually true becomes evident. When one UK poll asked respondents to identify the types of people they thought of when asked to identify 'migrants', the most popular answer (chosen by 62% of those asked) was 'asylum seekers'. Less than one third of respondents saw international students as 'migrants'. Yet students are the largest single group of migrants arriving in the UK, making up 37% of the total in 2009. In the same year, asylum seekers accounted for just 4% of the total number of migrant arrivals.[20]

Another difficulty is the preoccupation of the public with the incoming rather than the outgoing. Despite the fact that migration is a two-way process – that every *im*migrant is also an *e*migrant – our discussions about migration in developed countries are almost exclusively debates about immigration. But emigration is not a one-way flow: Western citizens leave their home countries too. There are an estimated 2.2 million British citizens living in the EU alone. Over 5.6 million British citizens live permanently abroad. In 2013, nearly 400 British citizens left the UK every day.[21] Patterns of migration are changing: countries like Nigeria, India and South Sudan, traditionally thought of as 'sending' countries, are increasingly destination points too.

But 'migrant' is a label that doesn't just speak to geography: it is also about class. Emigrants from the West, especially when highly skilled, are often identified – and identify themselves – not as 'immigrants' but 'expats'. As Leila Lalami, a Moroccan-American writer, has commented: 'You're a "migrant" when you're very poor; "immigrant" when you're not so poor; and "expat" when you're rich'.[22] If you type the two terms into a Google image search, photos of 'expats' show wealthy white wives shopping, drinking and sunbathing on the beach. 'Migrants' are poor: the photos online are of time spent queuing at borders, waiting in camps, and protesting against exploitation.

All this suggests that words matter. Something vital is being lost in translation when we talk about 'migrants' in undifferentiated terms: 'migrant' becomes an undesirable slur. Imagining immigrants as Romanian gypsies and Somali asylum seekers feeds on stock images and exaggerated stereotypes to present 'migration' as a threat to order and security, because migration is equated with poverty.

But it's not just about who migrants are: it's also about how many. In early 2014, I spent a few months asking nearly everyone I met across the UK how many people in Britain today they thought were migrants. Their guesses varied wildly, from 5% to 50%. The guesses averaged out at 30%. This straw poll echoes the findings of much more rigorous studies, including the 2011 Transatlantic Trend Survey.[23] In the UK, when asked to estimate the numbers of those resident who hadn't been born in the country, respondents answered that on average just under one-third (or 31.8%) of British residents were immigrants. In the US, the average estimate was higher – over one-third (37.8%). Across all the European countries surveyed, the average guess was 26%.[i]

These are gross overestimates. The UK's 2011 census suggests that the proportion of foreign-born British residents is closer to 13%: this is the same as in the US. Although there is significant regional variation, across the EU's member states 9.4 % of residents are foreign born. Across the West, the public consistently

---

[i] This figure includes EU citizens born in one member state and residing in another (e.g. a British citizen living in France), who account for about one-third of the EU's 'foreign born' residents.

overestimate the number of immigrants in their country by a factor of nearly three.[24] Poll after poll shows that the average Briton or American clearly thinks that there are too many migrants. But the same polls show that they also believe there to be almost three times the number of immigrants *than are actually here*.

This isn't just a Western problem. In 2009, as catastrophic failures of governance in Zimbabwe led to economic collapse, hundreds of thousands of Zimbabweans journeyed to South Africa, primarily in search of work. Estimates of up to four, six even ten million Zimbabweans roaming South African began to circulate in the mainstream press. However as Tara Polzer, a senior researcher at the University of Witwatersrand, pointed out at the time, these numbers could not possibly be true. Zimbabwe's total population is 12 million, 5 million of whom are children under 15. This did not mean that there was not a serious crisis in South Africa's asylum system: impoverished Zimbabweans were undoubtedly moving into South Africa. But turning hundreds of thousands into tens of millions did not help solve the problem: it only stoked fear.[25]

So what is the real scale of global migration? In 2013, according to the World Bank, there were 232 million people living outside the country of their birth.[26] This is a significant number: but it isn't overwhelming. Just 3% of the world's 7 billion inhabitants are international migrants. In global terms, this isn't much of a flood: it's more of a steady trickle. The real puzzle about the age of global mobility is arguably not why so many people are moving across borders, but why so many are *not*.

International migration is still not the norm. Most of us, if we move at all, do so within the borders of our own country – from Manchester to London, or from New York to California. In fact, we are at least six times *more* likely to migrate within a country (from one region to another) than we are to move across a border. There are at least 740 million domestic migrants, and yet these internal migrations are – for the most part – of little political consequence.[27] Few today would suggest we should restrict these migrations – in fact, the Universal Declaration of Human Rights explicitly prohibits such restrictions. But however obvious this may seem to us, your right to move within the borders of your own country has actually only been enshrined in law relatively recently. The US Supreme Court, for instance, only definitely confirmed US citizens' 'fundamental' right to 'move at will from place to place' across state lines in 1920.[28]

Even most international migrants do not go as far as the European, North American or Australasian publics often imagine. Forty percent of international migrants move to a neighbouring country.[29]   The Eastern European movements that have so preoccupied UK politicians in recent years reflect the fact that, at a global scale, most migration is regional. More than half of Africa's international migrants stay in Africa; the same regional preferences are reflected in the choices made by Asian and European migrants.[30] For the majority of the world's migrants, the West is not the only – not even the preferred – destination. Other similar migration stories are being written, too: from Dhaka to Delhi, and from Lusaka to Lagos.

These numbers are revealing, but they only tell us what migration *is*: not necessarily what it should be.

Nevertheless, migration numbers have a nasty habit of becoming migration targets. In 2010, David Cameron's Conservative Party promised to 'take steps to take net migration back to the levels of the 1990s – tens of thousands a year, not hundreds of thousands'.[31] In the ensuing four years, a raft of new restrictive migration policies – including imposing a cap of 20,700 on the total number of skilled non-EU workers who can enter Britain to take up a job with a salary of less than £150,000, cutting access to student visas, and introducing new minimum income tests for those seeking to sponsor a foreign spouse's arrival in the UK – have all been introduced with the explicit aim of driving down immigration from the record high of 252,000 in 2011.

However, despite an initial fall in the figures to just 153,000 in the year ending September 2012, the figure shot back up to 212,000 by the end of 2013.[32] The failure of the government's net migration drive is arguably evidence of the folly of trying to manage migration in crude quantitative terms.[33] But the policies introduced in the pursuit of this target underline that restricting migration necessarily involves making judgments about *who* should be allowed to migrate – and who shouldn't. Above all, it's the non-EU poor – the low-skilled and low-waged – who have been barred. Of course, adherents of such policies insist that such policies are 'good for Britain' and are about protecting the poor here, at home, from a race to the economic bottom. But we need to assess the evidence before we accept this assertion as truth.

Numbers can help frame patterns of migration, but they also help to reveal just how badly we comprehend the real dimensions and character of the immigration we're so frightened of, and hint at the extent to which those fears are about *poor* people moving. But to understand the relationship between immigration and inequality, we also need to think about principles. When is freedom of movement a right – and when is it a privilege?

3 PRIDE AND PATRIOTISM

Patriotism is, fundamentally, a conviction that a particular country is the best in the world because you were born in it.
George Bernard Shaw, *The World*, 15 November 1893

How far should freedom of movement extend? Few in the West would question the right of citizens to move freely in their own country, or their right to leave that country. In 2014, only a handful of mostly pariah countries still enforce strict exit-visa regulations – among them such places as Eritrea, North Korea and Uzbekistan. The Universal Declaration of Human Rights proclaims that 'everyone has the right to freedom of movement and residence within the borders of each state' and that 'everyone has the right to leave any country, including his own, and to return to his country'.[34] But beyond the border, human rights treaties offer only partial protection for freedom of movement. We may have the right to leave our own country, but we have no corresponding right to enter another. We also have the right to seek asylum, but not to be granted it.

This hardly seems 'fair'. But what most national politicians are trying to capture with the idea of 'fair' migration is something different – a sense that migrants' rights to arrive shouldn't trample the rights of those already here. In these terms, fairness doesn't lie in simply establishing a single set of rights, for migrants *or* for citizens: it lies in successful balancing the rights of migrants and the rights of others, so that one group's gains do not come at the expense of the other.

Thinking about global freedom of movement is nevertheless important when it comes to thinking about inequality, because the effects of birthplace upon life chances cannot be overstated. In 2012, the World Bank concluded that 'more than fifty percent of one's income depends on the average income of the country where a person lives or was born … a very large chunk of our income will be determined by only one variable, citizenship, that we generally acquire at birth'.[35] So where we are born determines to an enormous extent both how likely it is we are going to *need* to move, and also how free we will be to do so.

Inequality is largely determined at birth and is tied to geography. This means there's a powerful moral case for using migration as a means to remedy the arbitrary inequalities of birthplace that we usually conveniently ignore. The West's citizens cannot possibly claim that the riches that derive from our citizenship are fair: they are a fortunate accident of birth. So the real question we need to ask is: would more migration at least make things *fairer*?

Another way to ask this question is to inquire: who is migration good *for*? Most obviously, migration is clearly good for migrants. In particular, migrant poor from the Global South benefit from being able to move to more developed states. In 2009, the United Nations

Development Programme (UNDP) determined that migrants who moved from a low-income to a high-income country saw, on average, a 15-fold increase in income, a doubling of education enrolment rates and a 16-fold reduction in child mortality numbers.[36] Migration also benefits families and communities left behind. In 2014, the World Bank estimates that migrants from developing countries will collectively send $436 billion in remittances home, more than three times the total amount pledged as Official Development Aid. Yet, despite the growing body of evidence showing migration is good for development – and reduces global inequality – wealthy states are seeking to close their borders to low-skilled migration,[37] as studies show 'rising anti-immigrant sentiment' and increasing numbers of deportations.

In fact – as we'll see in Chapters 8 and 9 – there's a lot of evidence to suggest migration is also good for host communities. But before we concern ourselves with what's politically possible, we first need to determine what's *right*. So let's try an experiment. Forget existing migration policies: forget your own citizenship. Forget wealth, education, ethnicity. Philosopher John Rawls argued that in trying to decide what a fair society would look like, we needed to first draw a 'veil of ignorance' over own future life in that community.[38] If you design a 'fair' migration policy now, what would it look like? Are the people in this world free to move?

Almost certainly, your answer is yes. If we do not know whether we'll inherit privileges or not, we're unlikely to build a constitution that protects the elite. What looks 'fair' when we don't know whether we'll be rich or poor, American or African, is a system that provides the maximum possible equality of opportunity. Freedom of movement is a vital part of that.

This might appear to be an open-and-shut case. Migration offers a means of redressing chance inequalities: a counter to unearned birthplace privilege. How can freedom of movement be wrong? But the effects are more complex. Migration – seeking not just to visit a place but to *live* in it – quite clearly places new demands on existing members of the community. So how much protection do disadvantaged nationals need – or deserve – against the arrival of newcomers?

Some think it is obvious we should care most about nationals. David Goodhart, for instance, writes of his disbelief that anyone could claim that, when it comes to reducing poverty, Britons owe more to Burundians than to Brummies. [39] Yet development economist Michael Clemens offers a different viewpoint: 'people assert that local inequality is worse than global inequality … but I just don't know why I should think that'. [40] If – as utilitarians would argue – 'the greatest happiness of the greatest number … is the measure of right and wrong', [41] measuring the impact of migration upon inequality is a question that cannot end at the border. Yet many people have an equally strong 'gut instinct' that nations matter, too. So can we believe in global justice *and* continue to believe that nations deserve protecting?

Nearly everyone can agree that nations – communities – are important. But to understand the extent to which nations need protecting against migration, we need to know *why* they matter – and, in particular, what protections nations offer against inequality and poverty. Part of why nations matter is undoubtedly is about culture and belonging. We are none of us 'unencumbered individuals', and national cultures play a role in shaping our identities. [42] While some UK critics of pro-migration advocacy dismiss members of the

Oxbridge-educated, left-leaning, London chattering classes (like me) as being entirely disconnected from 'national' culture, and therefore too quick to trade this for cappuccino-sipping cosmopolitanism, this is unfair. National identity is a chameleon: it looks very different in Islington than it does in Blackpool. But people in both places agree on its importance. National identities are fragmented and diffused by factors as innocuous as personal taste and as powerful as gender, class and generation. Ask a San Franciscan and an Alabaman what it means to be an American, and the chances are you'd get very different answers. Even if they might agree on some basic principles of the American Way of Life – the self-evident truths about mankind's equality and the pursuit of happiness – if you try to flesh these ideas out, one legalises gay marriage while the other repeals gun control. Yet both pledge allegiance to the same flag.[43]

However the infinite variety of ways in which national identities are interpreted also suggests that a notion of 'national culture', *in and of itself*, isn't a justification for why we need nation-states – let alone why we should restrict migration. Ultimately, in liberal democracies, beneath the national paraphernalia of firework shows and barbecues on public holidays, beyond mealtimes and manners, our 'ways of life' are founded on *inclusive* rather than exclusive values. And first among these values are tolerance and justice: values that are open to migration.

Yet nation-states are more than just culture. Modern nations are also about citizenship – what Hannah Arendt, refugee and philosopher, called the 'right to have rights' in our modern world.[44] Our political arrangements mean that the 'rights of man' are – in practice – the rights of a Norwegian, a Canadian, or an Afghan. And chief among the promises that Western citizenship makes is the guarantee of equality – not of outcome, but of opportunity. But against the promise of equality between citizens must be balanced the problem of inequality between *citizenships*. For while all men and women may be created equal, not all states are. Norway offers much more to its citizens than Afghanistan can.

Of course, it is important to recognise that all citizenships offers us only the 'fiction of equality'. Outcome and opportunity cannot be so easily separated. In 2007, the richest 1% of Americans owned 35% of the country's wealth. In the UK, the wealthiest 1% is 215 times wealthier than the poorest 10% of Britons.[45] This explains why most worries about migration focus upon its possible effects on the poor – those whose citizenship offers them limited protection and less privilege.

Here, we come both to the crux of the argument for migration as a form of global justice and also to the most persuasive progressive case for national borders. Many in favour of tightly restricting migration would argue that it is *national* social rights – a historical pact between the wealthy and the workers – which really make national citizenship meaningful. They would also argue that borders are necessary to protect these social systems, because borders protect community cohesion and fiscal income. This is the nation-state not – in Goodhart's words – as a 'mystical attachment', but the institutional arrangement that can consistently deliver the democratic, welfare and psychological outcomes that most people, when given a choice, seem to want.[46]

In these terms, nation-states matter because they protect a real, tangible commitment to citizens' equality. This entails recognising that we have special responsibilities for our fellow-nationals' wellbeing. At one level, this is not so strange. Nearly all of us, for instance, care more about our family members' wellbeing than that of our acquaintances. Arguably, favouring locals is an extension of this – recognition that being part of a national community cements closer ties, so a fellow-citizen's wellbeing matters more than that of a stranger. [47] This is not altruism but self-interest: as members of a community, we have a vested interest in ensuring other members do not become undue burdens, draining our shared resources and disturbing our peace.

Yet all special relationships have their limits. A claim for special *protection* from harm is fair: but this is not the same as demanding *privilege*. The trick is to determine when national solidarity turns into nepotism. Rights of inheritance, 'special' family bonds and Old Boys' Networks entrench a great deal of privilege and power in our communities. But few would claim that the fact that the Prime Minister (David Cameron), Mayor of London (Boris Johnson) and Archbishop of Canterbury (Justin Welby) all attended the same public school, Eton, and are the sons of wealthy families, is a reflection of 'fairness' within the UK.

'Protection, not privilege' is therefore a good maxim around which to build a 'fair' migration policy. Our fellow citizens should be protected from harm, but providing this condition is met, it is hard to justify locking international migrants out. If we do, our interest in protecting what are essentially inherited privileges – that 50% lifetime birthplace bonus – against the huddled masses begins to look pretty selfish. At some point, it's no longer self-preservation, but greed.

The ethical contest between freedom of movement and nationalism can ultimately be understood as a struggle to balance competing versions of equality. For progressives, migration can best be defended when it works in the interests of global justice, pulling people out of poverty and redistributing wealth. This means immigration has to include the poor. But nationalism is *also* best defended when it binds a community together in pursuit of social justice, a social union able to counter neo-libertarians' headlong rush towards inequality. These are practices that demand a border be drawn *somewhere*. So the empirical challenge is to work out what balance between nationalism and migration – equality between citizens and equality between citizenship – best serves to maximise protection and minimise privilege for those on *both* sides of our borders.

4 FORTRESS EUROPE

EU Immigration has left the white working class effectively as an underclass, and that I think, is a disaster.
Nigel Farage, EU Debate with Nick Clegg, 2 April 2014

We've seen that building a fair migration system depends upon balancing global justice and national solidarity – maximising equality of opportunity on both sides of the border. But exactly where does that border lie? In the past hundred years we have come to recognise internal freedom of movement as a basic right. We insist, in the shadow of Bosnia's or Baghdad's sectarian wars, that no neighbourhood or town should be able to exclude citizens from moving there. Our urban spaces are no longer walled citadels, but when it comes to national borders, we're more conservative. Yet in Europe, EU citizenship represents a fundamental challenge to these older boundaries.

Today, all citizens of EU member states have the right to travel, reside and work in any other member state without discrimination." This is truly remarkable: 475 million EU citizens can migrate freely across 27 member states. Thanks to the Schengen Area's dismantling of internal border controls, European citizens can now travel from Helsinki to Lisbon without having to show a passport.[48] So is the European Union's guarantee of citizens' 'fundamental freedom' to move across 28 member states a bold experiment, establishing vital geographic and social mobility? Or is it simply a redrawing of the borders – so that perhaps Fortress Europe does not fight inequality but reinforces it?

On a Saturday in October, low sunlight throws long shadows over parked cars and Victorian terraces. Nothing could appear more English: quiet, unassuming London suburbia. But we're here today to celebrate something altogether different: the 10-year anniversary of our friend Ania's arrival in the UK. Ania is just one of a hundred thousand Polish immigrants who have made London their home in the past decade. Like many of these new Eastern European migrants, she initially only planned to stay in Britain for a year, to improve her English. Ten years later, Ania teaches English literature to Enfield's teenagers.

Inside the party, Union Jack bunting hangs from the ceiling: on the walls are photos of famous Poles and the odd British royal: Chopin, Pope John Paul II, Prince Charles. Ania is frying *pierogi* in the kitchen. Later, there's vodka. It's a haphazard, happy, multicultural mix.

Face-to-face with Ania – a young middle-class mother and teacher – a pejorative label like 'immigrant'

ⁱⁱ Transitional controls are still in place for citizens of Croatia, who will not have full freedom to work across the EU until 2018.

seems inappropriate: a world away from the clichés of Polish plumbers and Romanian gypsies. Yet Ania certainly counts herself as Polish when she reads in the newspapers about arson attacks in Belfast,[49] or hears abuse in the street. It's virtually impossible for her to ignore such widespread hostility. As the *Daily Express* crowed in January 2014, polling results show widespread anger directed towards Europeans who can arrive without visas: '79% say we must ban EU migrants'.[50]

This hostility towards Eastern European migrants is widespread, and hinges upon – among other things – the perceptions that poor EU migrants are stealing Western Europe's jobs. If freedom of movement is a key weapon in the fight against inequality, progressive politicians interested in social justice should surely welcome the removal of costly barriers to intra-European migration. So what does EU migration mean for inequality? We can break this question down into two parts. First, does freedom of movement help redress inequalities within Europe? Second, does EU migration exacerbate inequality within the UK – or for British citizens?

Given that 475 million European Union citizens have the right to migrate freely across the continent, what is actually striking is that so few have chosen to do so. Fourteen million EU citizens currently live in another member state – 2.5% of the EU's total population.[51] But when EU citizens *do* move, they predominantly go from East to West. Eighty percent of all mobile EU citizens who are of working age live in the UK, France, Germany, Spain or Italy. Since 2008, a new migration wave from South to North has crested, as citizens in Greece, Spain and Italy look to escape mass unemployment and stringent austerity measures at home through emigration.[52]

EU freedom of movement offers these European citizens a chance to leave behind stagnant economies, graduate unemployment and inefficient states to seek a better standard of living. Average wages in Poland are around a quarter of average UK wages: even a minimum-wage job in Britain pays more.[53] But it is not just about levelling up in terms of income: it is also about seeking out opportunities lacking in eastern Europe, where graduate unemployment rates hover at 20%. Many of the businesses and jobs that have been created in the past decade rely upon remittances: Poles sent $1.143 billion (about £730 million) back home from the UK in 2012.[54] Concerns have been raised about the extent to which emigration is an 'easy fix' that allows eastern European states to ignore deeper economic malaise, but it is clear that it is the principle of *free* movement that protects eastern Europe from the worst effects of brain drain and demographic decline, as migrants are able to move for short periods and return home regularly, rather than settling permanently.

European migration, in other words, brings EU migrants greater wealth and greater equality of opportunity. And it's vital to remember that *Britons are EU migrants too.* 2.3 million EU citizens live in the UK: but at least 2.2 million British citizens live elsewhere in the Europe, making Britain the largest exporter of people across the European Union.[55] Despite the stereotype of Briton's EU migrants as sunburnt monoglot retirees, only about 20% are pensioners. The rest – like the Europeans who come to the UK – are workers, students and spouses, looking for a better life.

Some politicians, such as Conservative MP Mark Field, have attempted to argue that British migrants are different from Europeans arriving in the UK, claiming that these are 'successful people living in second homes in Spain or France', and that 'most Brits living abroad are not aggressive beggars or sleeping rough on the streets'.[56] The data shows such claims are not just inflammatory but inaccurate. Perhaps more importantly, Field's comments reveal a view of migration as something that should be restricted to the wealthy and 'successful' – and, by implication, suggests that the real problem is the ability of the EU's poor to move freely, too.

Migration across Europe has helped to accelerate eastern European growth, and provided a lifeboat for the jobless graduates of southern Europe. Yet it is often alleged that this has happened at the expense of national working classes. So does protecting the poor here means keeping other poor out? Deep suspicions are expressed about the motivations of unskilled migrants arriving travelling west, with accusations made that their interest lies in taking advantage of existing social welfare systems without making a contribution. EU migrants in the UK must now show they have been earning £150 per week for three months before they can claim benefits. Germany has expressed similar concerns about poor and unskilled eastern Europeans, and migrants there will now have just three months to find a job there before facing deportation.[57]

If 'benefits tourism' is a real problem, such measures seem reasonable. European freedom of movement began as freedom of movement for *workers*. Deliberately moving to take advantage of social safety nets elsewhere can hardly be defended as 'fair use' of EU freedom of movement rights. Yet this is a big 'if'. Researchers at UCL showed in 2009 that so-called A8 migrants in the UK – migrants from the eight Baltic and eastern European low-income countries that joined the EU in

2004[58] – are 60% less likely than natives to receive state benefits or tax credits, and 58% less likely to live in social housing.[59] The accusations are without foundation: there is almost no evidence that eastern Europeans are migrating in search of state handouts rather than work.[60]

While – as we'll see later – there is some evidence to show that local low-skilled workers may suffer as a result of non-EU low-skilled migration, there's no record of any similar effect resulting from *European* migration. This is partly because EU migrants are free to move – and so can more easily arrive in economic boom and leave in economic bust than those who fear that, if they go, they will never find their way back. EU migrants can also work legally, reducing their dependency on exploitative employers willing to undercut the legal labour market. So, in fact, it's giving EU migrants more freedom to move – not less – which has protected local workers.

Nevertheless, the European Union's freedoms are undoubtedly capitalist freedoms: the peace it secured after World War II is a free-market peace. This helps explain why – despite the fact that today Euroscepticism is most closely associated with right-wing politics in the tradition of Margaret Thatcher – it has traditionally been the left who feared the advance of the European project. A closer examination of Europe's four freedoms suggests that the way in which these are being used by some businesses may indeed be undermining workers' social rights – and also adding to inequity between capital and labour.

As part of guaranteeing fair access to the EU's single market for companies, EU legislation allows employees from a company that has successfully bid for work abroad to be 'posted' there for up to two years. Today, there are estimated to be 1.2 million posted workers on short-term contracts in the EU. Although their pay must match minimum wages or collective trade agreements in the host state, a loophole means that an employer's social contributions (pensions, sick pay, holiday) can be paid in the worker's country of origin.

In France – where there are up to 200,000 posted workers – an EU contractor using Romanian or Latvian labourers can save up to 30% on high French labour costs, in a practice that has come to be labelled there as 'social dumping'.[61] In effect, this allows businesses to evade paying for workers' social rights – and often leaves the workers themselves with less stringent protections. The issue hit the headlines in Britain when in January 2009 workers at the East Lindsey Oil Refinery went on strike, demanding 'British Jobs for British Workers'. The French company Total, operating the refinery, had subcontracted an Italian company to provide services using posted Portuguese and Italian workers. British workers were not eligible to apply for these jobs.[62]

As a result of public outcry and trade union pressure, in December 2013 the EU agreed a new Posted Workers Enforcement Directive.[63] However trade unions have argued that this draft is still a 'shoddy compromise' that fails to address the issue of how to ensure 'free movement of labour works without a race to the bottom.' [64] The ferocity with which the UK government has fought against EU migration – with promises to revise the 'fundamental freedoms' at the heart of the EU charter to curtail European migration – thus makes it surprising that the same UK Government has been equally vehement in its opposition to any such reform of the Posted Workers system. In this case, protecting British workers from being undercut by migrants has been judged less important than protecting the 'competitiveness' of British businesses in the single market.[65]

The European Union's supporters are quick to point to the benefits of free movement for 500 million Europeans – more rights, more opportunities, more choice. UKIP and other anti-European parties are equally quick to point to free movement as European perfidy, as EU immigrants undercut local workers' pay. But look beyond the EU's borders, and Europe's migration policies look distinctly *il*liberal. For the Europe that guarantees its citizens' mobility is the same Europe set on keeping others out. The dismantling of Britain's borders has occurred in parallel with the building of a new Fortress Europe.[66]

Borders are always protectionist: someone is always excluded, and that someone is usually poor. Greater equality between Europeans has come at the expense of wider global freedom of movement. Having opened up a pan-European labour market, the immediate need to recruit low-skilled workers from further afield – from the developing economies of African and Asia – is relatively limited. The poorer economies that stretch from the Baltic to the Balkans already provide an ample pool of European labourers willing to take on manual work.

As a result, Europe spends €2 billion protecting the Fortress' walls from interlopers every year. Frontex, the European Border Agency for External Security, is headquartered in Warsaw, Poland. Established in 2004, its role is to coordinate border management across the European Union – relying upon equipment and staff seconded from national governments to seal Europe's borders.[67] At the height of the Arab Spring in February 2011, for instance, Frontex put into effect Operation

Hermes, which aimed to detect – and to deter – African migrants from crossing the Mediterranean.

The results of Frontex's industry must be measured not just in money spent, or illegal crossings detected – some 25,000 in 2013, an average of one every four hours – but in migrants dead. At least 20,000 would-be migrants are thought to have died on the Mediterranean sea in the past 20 years trying to reach Europe, as smugglers pack leaky boats and coastguards are accused of looking the other way. Numerous human rights advocates have warned that Frontex's operations have blocked refugees from being able to apply for vital protection, as is their right under international – and EU – law.[68] One recent study found that 80% of those intercepted by the Italian navy's 'Mare Nostrum' operation had grounds for claiming asylum.[69]

Yet despite brief bursts of collective conscience – as in October 2013 when 363 migrants drowned off the coast of Lampedusa, Italy – Europe's politicians appear committed to continuing to meet this humanitarian crisis with deterrence. So while the dead of the Lampedusa shipwreck were posthumously awarded Italian citizenship, the survivors were detained and deported.[70] The poor and the persecuted, after all, are less dangerous when they're dead.

In the end, the fears of European politicians about both external and internal freedom of movement are – above all – fears about the poor being able to move freely. In late 2013, the British government raised the possibility that citizens of new EU member states should only be permitted to move freely to the UK once GDP per capita in their own country reached 75% of British levels.[71] Aside from the fact that by any similar measure Britons would be barred from migrating to Sweden,

Switzerland or Norway, the reasoning behind the proposal is revealing. This is not about stopping Europeans from moving: it's about stopping *poor* Europeans from moving.

Thus, fighting to reverse EU freedom of movement isn't about simply protecting 'our' poor from nefarious Bulgarian builders, or stopping Syrian refugees – re-labelled as 'illegals' and 'terrorists' once they try to cross the Mediterranean – from arriving here. It's about transforming freedom of movement from a 'right for the worker to raise her or his standard of living', to a freedom dependent upon the interests of employers and profit-seeking capital. As backbench Labour MP Jon Trickett complained in 2008, this suggests that when it comes to considering free movement across the EU, we're actually having the wrong debate – one about 'the nation-state as opposed to the superstate', rather than discussing whether we want 'a liberal Europe as opposed to a social Europe.'[72]

The European free-movement project is fraught with contradictions. It has brought enormous opportunity for millions of European citizens: but the costs have been paid above all by those would-be migrants beyond Europe's borders, many of whom are seeking not work but sanctuary. EU free movement is also a free-market project – it's as much about growth as equity. This helps to explain why there's no apparent contradiction in the fact that, for some companies, Europe's newly reinforced borders are very good for business indeed.

5 THE MIGRATION INDUSTRY

Immigrants are fast becoming the modern day cash crop in the prison industry.

J. Green and S. Patel, *Briefing Materials Submitted to the United Nations Special Rapporteur on the Human Rights of Migrants,* 2007

When we talk about immigration and inequality, we tend to focus on the immigrants who have already arrived. But the very act of migrating – negotiating visas, crossing the border – is inextricably shaped by the profits that can be made from enforcing – or evading – the rules and regulations intended to keep the poor in their places.

Modern migration is a billion-dollar industry. From the torn posters stapled to telegraph poles in every African city I've ever visited – 'Want a Work Permit in SA? Call this number' – to the black-tie ticketed cocktail receptions at which immigration lawyers explain to those with money how they can negotiate immigration rules to their advantage, there's money to be made moving people.

This Migration Industry is most visible at the border. In June 2013, the US Senate passed an Immigration

Reform Bill (which later stalled in Congress) only after it was agreed to allocate an additional $38 billion to improve border security with Mexico. A total of $46 billion dollars was to be spent on border security, so that 20,000 new law-enforcement officials could police 350 new miles of fence. As Forbes Magazine reported, the bill 'offer[ed] a bonanza of cash for the defence industry … mandating the purchase of everything from helicopters to night vision goggles to drones'.[73]

The US is not the only Western state spending billions literally barricading itself against an immigrant onslaught. Fences separate the Spanish North African enclaves of Cueta and Melilla from Morocco, Uzbekistan from Turkmenistan and Afghanistan, Saudi Arabia from Yemen, Botswana from Zimbabwe, and China from North Korea: all built in the name of deterring illegal immigrants. Israel is currently spending upwards of $270m to build a two-layer fence completely sealing the 266km Egypt-Israeli border, in the hope of deterring the irregular immigrants from crossing via Egypt from Sudan and Eritrea.[74] Although there are only around 60,000 African asylum seekers and refugees (Israel's total population is just under 8 million), proponents of draconian laws aimed at cutting off African migration – including Israeli Interior Minister Eli Yishai – argue that the 'Zionist dream' is at risk because 'there are millions there [in Eritrea and Sudan] who, God forbid, might be murdered. Should we open our gates to all of them?'[75] Each fence is a visible reminder that migration policies are designed to exclude as well as include – and that, in a capitalist economy, there are profits to be made doing both.

For the Migration Industry, migration is a commercial transaction. The push to secure our collective national borders has been outsourced to private, profit-seeking firms. The irony does not stop there. These corporations' complex commercial interests and future profitability depend upon continued facilitation of the free movement of capital across the globe – while their business models rely upon governments placing increasing restriction on the free movement of people across borders.

The names of the Migration Industry powerhouses are familiar multinational behemoths. G4S – a British-based 'security solutions' company – is the third-largest private-sector employer in the world, with 650,000 employees and offices in 125 states. In the UK, G4S currently runs two immigration-removal centres, including Brook House at Gatwick Airport, a purpose-built 426-bed centre with security measures equivalent to those found in a Category B prison.[76] Multinational corporation Serco – 100,000 employees in 30 countries and revenues in 2013 totalling $4.9 billion dollars – also runs two detention centres in the UK, including the notorious Yarl's Wood and Colnbrook detention centres, where repeated allegations of abuse have been made by detainees.[77] A third key player in the British migration industry, Reliance Secure Task Management, was rebranded Tascor after acquisition by the outsourcing giant Capita PLC for $31.6m in 2012. Since 2010, Tascor has held the contract for the supervision of deportations from the UK, escorting and removing 18,000 individuals each year – a contract previously held by G4S, but lost shortly after the unlawful killing of Angolan deportee Jimmy Mubenga in 2010 during a G4S-supervised deportation.[78]

This expansion of private-service provision in the interests of 'securing our national borders' is a global phenomenon. In 2009, Serco won a contact to provide Australia with immigration detention services at 17 locations on the mainland, and on Christmas Island. Initially valued at $370m, the contract quickly ballooned to $756m as the number of immigration detainees increased sixfold from 1,000 to over 6,700.[79]

In the US, G4S has been responsible for escorting illegal migrants back from the US to Mexico since 2006, when the US Customs and Border Protection Agency decided to outsource this 'vital service'. Other major players in the US Migration Industry include the Florida-based company GEO, which controls 7000 out of 32,000 immigration detention beds in America, and the Corrections Corporation of America (CCA), which owns and manages 60 private prisons and has spent over $17m lobbying US government officials for stricter enforcement of custodial sentences – which, for the CCA, means additional income. Immigration is a fast-growing market for the CCA: the numbers of migrants incarcerated in the US have tripled in the past decade, to a daily average of 33,000, and for-profit companies now hold 50% of these detainees in privately operated centres.[80]

For the vast majority of those detained, there is no evidence to suggest that imprisonment is in the public interest. In fact, research has shown that alternatives to immigration detention – including release on bail, community supervision and regular reporting – all of which have been trialled in places including Australia, Belgium and Canada – can cost 95% less than detention. They also have extremely high rates of compliance and are better able to meet international human rights standards.[81] But while detention often isn't necessary, it's certainly profitable.

The choices that states have made to privatise the delivery of those 'secure borders' have turned migration into an industry that is governed not by principles of right and wrong, but the economics of profit and loss. As the UK Home Affairs Select Committee pointed out to the Managing Director of G4S and Chief Executive of Serco in June 2013, 'the fact of the matter is that you are in the business … to make profit one way or the other'. Both executives immediately agreed.[82]

The world of outsourced government services is one in which private profits are often equated with public savings. In 2012, Serco, G4S and Tascor were awarded contracts to supply housing for asylum seekers across six regions worth up to £1.1 billion in revenue. The main objective of the outsourcing was 'to reduce the cost of asylum support', saving the Home Office £140 million. For government austerity to align with private profit, however, cost savings had to be made, either by 'procuring much poorer accommodation in less desirable areas, or by using the accommodation more intensively'.[83]

This underlines the ugly economic realities of the Migration Industry. Profit margins are often low. In 2013, Serco's Chief Executive claimed that it made just 21p per asylum seeker accommodated per day, but had chosen to enter the space because for Serco 'accommodation management [is] an important development area'.[84] Such low financial margins, however, come with human costs. Within months of these companies taking on the accommodation contracts, charities and local government associations began raising concerns about the poor quality of housing offered – providing evidence that tenants were suffering from pest infestations, a lack of heating and hot water, windows and doors that could not be locked, and a failure to provide basic amenities such as cookers or sinks. [85]

The asylum housing controversy in the UK is just one example of a corporate culture in which 'migration management' has resulted in the neglect and abuse of migrants. In Australia, riots among detainees on Manus Island left one dead and thirteen injured, with asylum seekers claiming to have seen G4S guards stamping on the skull of the young Iranian who suffered fatal head injuries, while other asylum seekers were beaten with iron bars and racially abused.[86] In the UK, three G4S guards are now standing trial for the manslaughter of Jimmy Mubenga, who suffocated when restrained on a plane en route to Angola from Heathrow.[87]

It is important to recognise that the Migration Industry is not just about corporate profit – it is also about workers' wages. In much the same way that British weapons factories that produce arms to be sold to Saudi Arabia and other allies are justified as 'entirely legitimate' because 'that is an important thing for jobs in this country',[88] border patrols, detention facilities and visa processing employ tens of thousands of citizens, often for low wages and in geographically marginalised areas. In March 2014, Exeter University researcher Jenny Allsopp investigated local responses to the imminent opening of a new immigration detention centre in Weymouth, an area of high unemployment where job opportunities are scarce. She found a community in which immigration detention was above all framed as an employment issue. Locals expressed relief at new jobs for some of the staff laid off from two recently closed prisons. As Allsopp relates, 'everyone "knows someone who knows someone" who will work at the Verne … it's all about jobs. And that is something that a lot of anti-deportation campaigns have missed'.[89]

However the Migration Industry is no model employer. The jobs it provides are overwhelmingly low paid and precarious: the workers do not share in the profits generated by this industry. Unions have consistently produced evidence that employees of companies like G4S and state border agencies like United Kingdom Border Agency (UKBA)[iii] are often poorly trained, as well as constrained by unresponsive management structures that deliberately foster cultures of hostility.[90] Thus in offering much-needed local employment, but with poor pay and conditions, the Migration Industry actually *entrenches* local inequality, taking advantage of immobility in socially marginalised and geographically isolated communities.

Of course, the legal Migration Industry's mantras of compliance, regulation and control only make sense set against the backdrop of the migration black market. It's important to recognise that smugglers and security firms have a symbiotic relationship. Both groups make their profits from the restrictions placed on immigration – one enforcing the law, one helping to break it.

Human trafficking is undoubtedly one of the most evil of all crimes, involving the moving of individuals by coercion, abduction or deception for the purposes of exploitation – whether for slavery, prostitution, forced labour, or even the removal of organs. The ILO

[iii] The United Kingdom Border Agency was the executive agency in charge of border control in the UK from 2008 to 2013. In 2013, following a damning report into the Agency's work, UKBA was abolished and its work returned to the Home Office.

estimates that there are at least 2.45 million trafficking victims in the world today: four-fifths are women, and the US Government estimates that, of these, up to two-thirds are sexually exploited.[91] The value of the market in sexual exploitation alone is at least $3 billion a year: total illicit profits from trafficked persons are likely to exceed $32 billion.[92]

Stories of women drugged and kept under lock and key, forced to prostitute themselves and deprived of all earnings, are truly horrific. Outrage is the only reasonable response. But to interpret the whole migration black market as trafficking is to misread it – and to ignore the extent to which smuggling is in part a response to the prohibitive cost of legal migration.[93] Most of the irregular migrants who cross borders illegally are not actually trafficked. They have *consented* to be smuggled across the border, knowingly breaking the law to 'invest everything in the hope of forthcoming remittances'.[94]

The smuggling market is worth at least $6.75 billion annually, based on calculations looking only at the principal smuggling routes from South to North America and Africa to Europe.[95] An Afghan may pay $25,000 to reach London, a Bangladeshi $10,000 to arrive in Brazil. Many migrants incur heavy debts and onerous social obligations as a result of the cost of their journey, as they borrow the money to migrate and are then expected to send back remittances and support their backers indefinitely. The risks are considerable. At least 1500 would-be migrants perished on the Mediterranean Sea in 2011, the deadliest year on record, and last year a record 500 died on the US-Mexico border.[96]

Yet total remittances to developing countries amounted to at least $414 billion in 2013. While legal migrants send the vast majority of this money,[97] there can be little doubt that irregular migrants are, collectively, sending billions back home every year. That's why so many Somalis, Afghans, Mexicans and other poor citizens are willing to risk death on the high seas or in the Sonoran desert: irregular immigration can make economic sense. In some cases, the cost and administrative hassle of obtaining legal authorisation can even make irregular migration a *cheaper* option. Research carried out jointly by the International Labour Organisation and UNHCR in 2008, for instance, found that for Afghans seeking work in Iran it was cheaper and quicker to hire a smuggler for an average cost of $361 – which they could expect to pay back after working for a few months – than to pay $640 to apply for an official visa that – even if it were approved – would anyway expire after three months.[98]

Looking at the people who manage migration helps to underline just how embedded the migration business is in Western economic and political structures. The Migration Industry is part of a much wider low-wage economy delivering privatised 'public' services. But, ingeniously, in adopting the language of national security, the act of policing migration continually reaffirms the importance of 'state security' – even as the state itself is hollowed out. The result is that the business of migration is increasingly an ugly one. Private corporations profit from fear and restrictive legislation, with little evidence that such activities serve the public good rather than private interest. Building borders triggers an arms race between sinister smugglers and unsavoury security firms. The losers are both taxpayers and migrants, as the migration industry makes its profits enforcing inequality and making it more difficult to travel – unless you have money.

6 CITIZENSHIP FOR SALE

'My passports are just like my credit cards … I take out the one that's going to save me the most time, and cost me the fewest dollars.'
Dual-national discussing travel across Africa, November 2010

It is a hot morning in Kampala, the air already heavy with what will become the afternoon's storm clouds. [99] I am on the back of a *boda-boda*, on my way to meet a friend – and his passport broker. Uganda, like many other parts of the developing world, is a country awash with intermediaries, fixers, brokers. Almost everything is available for a fee: including official documents. Provided you can pass physically as a Ugandan national, you can buy a Ugandan passport for around $100 USD. This is about three times the official rate.

There is often a dark side to this grey economy. But the passport broker I meet in this hotel lobby, Faith, [100] is a sunny middle-aged lady, whose yellow eyeshadow matches her manicured nails. She used to work in the civil service: her husband is a lawyer. She offers to help Patrice – a Congolese refugee – negotiate a Ugandan passport as a favour for an old friend (they used to work together).

After all 'this is all just paperwork. I know him, I trust him. And if he's got the money, why shouldn't he be able to travel?'

A world away from Kampala, Henley & Partners are a different sort of migration broker. Their publicity materials exude wealth, privilege and exclusivity. The firm – which describes itself as the 'world's leading specialists in citizenship planning' – is registered in the Channel Islands and has offices in twenty-two countries. Their website offers a comprehensive list of reasons why 'in an unsettled, ever-changing world, acquiring a second citizenship is a wise decision and an investment for the future'. As the website's link to a newspaper article on the Mumbai terror attacks reminds us, there may be times when even an American or a British passport is a serious liability.[101]

Henley & Partners offer to facilitate – for processing fees that usually begin at US $35,000 for a single applicant, and a commission on the purchase price – citizenship by investment. Invest in approved real estate (beach condos) in the right Caribbean paradise – or donate a six-figure sum to the state's development fund – and you can have a shiny new passport. This is a very different idea of citizenship.[102]

Such economic citizenship – the exchange of cash for a new passport in pursuit of more 'personal freedom, privacy and security' – is entirely legal. Henley & Partners hold marketing fairs worldwide, extolling the virtues of citizenship-by-purchase. Their price point may be very different from Faith's, but their philosophy is essentially the same. If you are lucky enough to have a spare $500,000, but by an unfortunate accident of birth are a wealthy citizen in a poor or ostracised state (such as Iran or Palestine), why shouldn't you be able to travel?

Every year, Henley & Partners release a 'Visa Restriction Index' that ranks countries according to how many places their citizens can visit without needing to apply for a visa. In 2013, Finland, Sweden and the UK topped the list, with their citizens able to travel to 173 states visa-free, followed closely by other wealthy OECD states.[103] At the bottom of the Henley & Partners' list we find poverty and conflict: Afghanistan (visa-free access to 28 countries); Iraq (31); Somalia and Pakistan (32). Those few dozen countries that will admit Afghans or Somalis without requiring extra screening and extra financial compensation are – for the most part – small island states, safe in the knowledge that geography and airline schedules make arrivals from Kabul or Baghdad unlikely: Haiti, Pitcairn, Palau, Tuvalu, and the Seychelles.[104]

Immigration is thus permeated by inequality. Citizenship acts as a kind of crude national wealth marker, allowing for collective discrimination. It is no accident that the ability to travel freely is both directly related to wealth and inversely proportionate to the likely *need* to migrate. Although of course it's possible to apply for a visa individually, the process is expensive and the decisions often arbitrary. We mistrust the global poor – who can't come as visitors, because we don't want them as migrants. Money is increasingly being used as a filter, facilitating the movement of the wealthy while blocking the movements of the majority. In 2013, the UK government announced plans to charge Indian, Nigerian, Sri Lankan and other 'high-risk' migrants a £3,000 bond for a six-month visa, ostensibly to reduce numbers overstaying after their visas expire. Following outrage at the 'discriminatory' proposal – and warnings that such bonds could derail UK trade with the fast-growing Indian and Nigerian economies – the policy was dropped. Yet the plan underlined how restrictive migration policies aren't about nationalism as much as wealth. Fines and fees are prohibitive for the poor: but the very ability to pay these sums gives the rich permission to move freely.

Of course, migration has always had an associated economic cost: there have always been tickets to buy, goods to ship, guides and fixers to pay. But the extent to which the *right* to migrate in now contingent upon economic wealth is unprecedented.

Outside free-movement zones such as the EU, legal migration is now hugely expensive. To come to the UK, it will cost you £278 to apply for a student visa and between £412 and £840 for a work visa. There are more fees if you're applying to settle permanently in the UK – £851 if it's as the spouse or civil partner of a UK citizen, £1,906 if you're the parent or grandparent. It's a further £874 to apply for naturalisation.[105] That's *before* the lawyers' fees, which usually run to four figures. In the US, legal fees run from around $2,000 for a temporary technical visa to up to $20,000 to obtain a 'green card' for permanent residency. Some Americans, including Chicago Mayor Rahm Emanuel, have also voiced concern that hard-working long-term legal migrants are effectively being 'priced out of citizenship': fees for naturalisation have tripled from $225 in 1999 to $685 in 2007. The Migration Policy Institute, a US think tank, reported in 2012 that one-fifth of those Latino immigrants who do naturalise in the US have to borrow money in order to do so.[106]

Putting a price on migration certainly keeps the poor out. But the emergence of a citizenship market does offer wealthy individuals the means to escape an arbitrarily assigned citizenship by paying for a passport that lets them travel. The Federation of Saint Christopher and

Nevis, better known as St Kitts and Nevis, is a tiny two-island Caribbean state with a population of just 53,000. Since 1984 it has run a citizenship-by-investment programme. In exchange for $400,000 in an approved real-estate purchase, or a $250,000 donation to the Sugar Industry Diversification Fund, you can become a St Kittsian passport holder in as little as four to six months.[107]

St Kitts' programme is the oldest citizenship-by-investment programme in existence, and remains the industry gold standard. The island of Dominica sets its price lower than St Kitts, at just $100,000 for a single applicant, and $200,000 for a family of four. New island states are entering the market too: both Antigua & Barbuda and Granada announced in 2013 that they would seek to establish citizenship-by-investment programmes.[108] So while former colonial status no longer qualifies you for preferential tariffs on sugar or bananas, many Caribbean states *are* able to command high prices for their passports because – as members of the Commonwealth – these documents unlock visa-free travel to the Western world. Facing high levels of debt, the ability to commoditise passports has become a valuable Caribbean resource.

What does it mean to be able to buy citizenship? On the one hand, market justice could be seen as offering an escape from the injustices of assigning citizenship by birth. But as we saw in Chapter 3, progressive nationalism is best defended when framed as the protection of a community of equals: putting a price on membership undermines this idea of solidarity. Furthermore, it appears selling citizenship compounds local inequality. St Kitts' citizenship programme is estimated to have brought at least USD $150 million to the islands, but the poverty rate remains stubbornly high, and inequality is growing.[109] The ability to create a class of wealthy, non-resident elite citizens has arguably weakened the state's need to account for its failings to local citizens – many of whom have in turn sought to escape economic inequality and stagnation through emigration.

Yet, despite this, the Citizenship Market is expanding. Western states are adopting similar programmes. In the US, EB5 visas provide access for investors (and their dependents) to visas in return for an investment of $1 million (or $500,000 in a rural area or place of high unemployment), which creates or preserves at least 10 jobs for US workers.[110] In the UK, placing £1 million in disposable income into a UK bank will secure a visa, and permanent residency after five years. The UK's Migration Advisory Committee (MAC) recently criticised the existing scheme for failing to set a *higher* price, and allowing money to be loaned rather than permanently invested. MAC recommended that the threshold should be raised to £2 million and a limited number of 'premium' fast-track visas auctioned off to the highest bidders.[111]

In 2012, Spain announced that permanent residency would be available to all those willing to invest €160,000 in the beleaguered Spanish property market – though the price tag has since been raised to €500,000, for fear Spain 'looked cheap'. Portugal and Ireland, fellow victims of the Eurozone recession, run similar schemes. Cyprus offers permanent residency for all those willing to spend €300,000 on property. The majority of applications come from the wealthy citizens of authoritarian states, especially Russia and China, looking to buy free movement.[112] In late 2013, Malta went a step further, passing controversial legislation that would allow it to sell EU citizenship to those willing to pay €650,000, despite the European Parliament condemning the scheme for turning citizenship into a 'tradable commodity'.[113]

Fundamentally, the problem with setting a price on citizenship is that it creates a two-tier system: one rule for those who can pay, one rule for those who can't. As a result, migration is no longer a great leveller: we've instead set up systems that compound inequality. Increasingly, the rules policing this system affect not only migrants, but average citizens too.

As the saying goes, love knows no borders. However, in July 2012, the British government introduced new family migration rules, requiring anyone wanting to sponsor their non-EEA (European Economic Area) spouse's visa for the UK to show that their annual income exceeded £18,600 (rising to £22,400 for a spouse and a child, with an additional £2,400 asked for every further child). Only the British partner's income can be counted – even if they're not the main breadwinner.[114] In related changes, elderly parents and grandparents who are non-EEA citizens can only be sponsored if you're able to show that it's impossible to obtain a required level of care in their home country – so even if you *can* meet the income requirement to sponsor your ageing parents' visas, you also have to show that you can't simply buy care for them abroad.

Those affected aren't paupers, just average families. In fact, 47% of the British public – and 60% of women – would fail to meet the minimum income required to sponsor a foreign relative into the country. Those barred from bringing in their foreign spouse include many who work in public-service jobs – as nurses and classroom assistants, or those training as teachers or veterinarians.

Talking to the men and women affected, their heartache is obvious. Douglas Shillinglaw, a self-employed mortgage broker in his 40s, tells me that he was never interested in politics before this. Now, politics consumes him. In 2012, The UKBA denied his Nigerian wife – the mother of his ten-month-old son – a visa to come and live in the UK, on the grounds that he could not prove his earnings reached the threshold necessary to support her. He can't just move to Nigeria: his 11 year-old son from a previous marriage lives in London. When I spoke to him in August 2013, his loneliness, anger and frustration were evident: 'How can the British government do this to me? I'm a British citizen: why can't I bring my family here?'.[115] Evidence from the British Medical Association suggests that, since July 2012, the NHS may have already lost some skilled doctors forced to emigrate in order to take care of their ageing parents. Harder to quantify is the number of British citizens who – living abroad – have chosen not to return to the UK because of these new family rules, effectively choosing exile over separation.[116]

While these newer, tougher rules may help the government reduce immigration numbers, it's not clear whether there's any public benefit as a result. In fact, researchers from Middlesex University have concluded that the government's policy may well end up *costing* the UK taxpayer $850m in the next decade, because UK citizens who have been left coping as single parents while their partners wait in immigration limbo are more likely to have to rely on benefits and less likely to be able to take up full-time employment.[117]

A market system makes the right to migrate dependent upon money: it sets the rich free, but leaves the poor – especially those poor both in terms of wealth and in terms of citizenship – doubly disenfranchised. However there are alternatives. One programme that stands in direct contrast to this new trend for buying and selling citizenship is the US 'Green Card Lottery'. Established in 1990, would-be migrants with a high-school education can apply for the chance to be interviewed for an American visa, provided no more than 50,000 of their countrymen have immigrated to the US in the past five years.[118] Nine million people entered the Lottery in 2013, hoping to be allocated one of 55,000 visas.[119] Compared to other migration systems that are designed to weed out the poor, the Diversity Visa Lottery stands out as offering relative equality of opportunity to all-comers: it is the main route for African migrants looking to arrive in the US. [120] But the Green Card lottery faces an uncertain future: lobbyists paid by large corporations keen to secure higher numbers of visas for highly-skilled migrants are prepared to trade in the Lottery for promises of labour-migration reform.[121]

Exploring the citizenship market thus underlines the extent to which migration is increasingly a rich man's game. Nevertheless, defenders of market-controlled migration are still quick to point to a humanitarian exception, enshrined in international law. Because, for some would-be migrants, legitimacy lies not in proving how *rich* but how *persecuted* you are. So while setting a price on legal movements may be selfish, it's surely not immoral: for, if you fear for your life or your freedoms, we will let you in. Won't we?

7 THE WRETCHED OF THE EARTH

Through the wire one last time observe
I am sewing my lips together
That which you are denying us
we should never have had to ask for.
    Mehmet Al Assad, *Asylum*, Borderlands 2002

There are some basic humanitarian principles that nearly all of us would defend. These include the right of every person to seek refuge from the worst of persecutions by crossing a border and claiming asylum. But it is harder to turn from principle to practice. Just how do you know who's a 'real' refugee, and who's a 'bogus' migrant? How do you ensure that protecting asylum rights doesn't open up a gap in the border for all-comers?

    The United Nations High Commission for Refugees (UNHCR) estimates that there are at least 16.7 million refugees worldwide.[122] Six and a half million refugees have spent more than five years in exile. Palestinians are not the only third-generation refugees: there are also tens of thousands of Somalis in Kenya, Afghans in Pakistan, and

Burundians in Tanzania who are not just the children but the *grandchildren* of the original refugees who fled violent conflict. To these 16.7 million refugees must be added at least another 33 million internally displaced persons (IDPs). In total, some 51.2 million men, women and children are currently displaced across the globe.[123]

Everyone wants to shelter these genuine refugees.[124] Even anti-immigration parties such as UKIP insist that they 'would allow genuine asylum applications': Nigel Farage has publicly urged the UK government to do more to accept Syrian refugees.[125] But far fewer seem to think they've actually *met* one, because, in the words of Phil Woolas, former UK Minister for Immigration, there's an equally strong conviction that 'most asylum seekers … are economic migrants'.[126]

The result is that reducing the number of asylum seekers arriving in the West has increasingly come to be seen as an important means of protecting the integrity of both the asylum and immigration systems. For instance, Australia's decision in July 2013 to refuse to allow any asylum seekers arriving by boat to settle in Australia (instead moving them to Papua New Guinea) was partly claimed to be an attempt to protect the rights of 'genuine refugees' in camps against nefarious 'queue-jumpers.[127] Public anger is directed against those foreigners 'cheating' the system, while preserving the idea that Australia, the UK – in fact, pretty much every country in the West – has a 'proud record' of welcoming and helping refugees.[128] Conveniently, this means that restricting asylum arrivals – in other words, reducing migration – can be presented as preserving equity of access to asylum.

In the popular mind, 'real' refugee crises are the ones we follow at a distance, 'giving generously' and then forgetting. On the tube trains in London, the Syria crisis becomes a picture of a screaming little girl next to the headline 'SYRIA CRISIS: DONATE NOW'. Two years ago, the girl was an emaciated Somali, and the camp flashed across our news bulletins was not Zaatari, Jordan, but Dadaab, Kenya. Before Dadaab, it was Haiti; before that, Darfur. There is always a crisis, always a crying baby, always another donation needed. The posters and the television packages reinforce one very obvious – and for many, a very comforting – truth: 'real' refugee crises do not happen here, but elsewhere, far away, over there.

We are certainly slow to draw connections between the asylum seekers we view with cynicism close to home (most likely in 2013 to be Afghans, Syrians or Serbians) and the victims on our television screens – even though many come from the same places. Over half (55%) of all refugees worldwide are the nationals of just five countries: Afghanistan, Somalia, Iraq, Syria and Sudan. Asylum seekers here thus come from the same place as 'real' refugees there.[129] Nevertheless, some commentators argue that that in the cold light of the twenty-first century, without Soviet guns trained inwards to keep refugees behind the iron curtain, we cannot afford the promise of asylum, that refugee protection is 'a kind of bluff designed to salve our consciences in a few well-publicised cases', a hypocrisy that has come back to haunt us because we never intended refugees to be able to actually *arrive* here.[130]

But arrive they do. In London, a taxi driver swings into the street, braking suddenly to avoid the headscarf-wearing pedestrian who has stepped out into the flow of traffic. He sighs. 'To be honest love, I just don't see why these asylum seekers all have to come here....' I fume silently in the back seat, angry not just at his words but at my own cowardice in being too polite, too passive – too

British – to challenge his conviction that we are faced with a swarm of asylum seekers, 'picking up hand-outs from the taxpayer in return for doing nothing'.

The average Briton thinks that the UK hosts 24% of asylum seekers, but the reality is that Britain is home to just under 1% of the world's refugees and asylum-seekers (about 150,000 people in total).[131] The overwhelming majority of refugees leave poor, insecure countries on foot, crossing into neighbouring states that are sometimes as poor and insecure as the places they left. The 49 least-developed countries – places like Chad, Malawi, and Yemen – provide asylum to 2.4 million refugees. The imbalance is growing. Ten years ago, developing countries hosted 70% of all refugees. Today in 2014, they are home to 86% of the world's refugees.[132] By whatever measure you choose, the idea that the West is under siege from would-be refugees flies in the face of statistical evidence. In Pakistan, there are 552 refugees for every dollar per capita GDP; the number is 303 in Ethiopia, and 301 in Kenya. For the US, UK and Australia, the equivalent numbers are 5.4, 4.7 and 0.9 respectively.[133] There is very little equity in the sharing of refugee populations: Western countries have become adept at burden-shifting.

Despite concerns that conflicts in Syria and Ukraine may be fuelling a new European asylum crisis, the number of asylum claims being made in the UK today is also considerably lower than in 2002, when – having risen rapidly through the 1990s – the number of asylum claims made peaked at 84,130. This prompted a slew of government measures designed to root out fraud and abuse, and thus soothe a worried public. The strategies employed to reduce asylum numbers were varied. Some – such as reducing benefit levels, removing access to labour markets, and speeding up the appeals process – were intended to eliminate the attraction of 'soft-touch Britain' and allow the swift removal of those who were trying to use the asylum system not to flee persecution, but because other avenues of migration were closed. However, in line with other traditional countries of refuge like Canada and Australia, British policies in the past decade have also placed an increasing focus upon *deterrence*: preventing the arrivals of any asylum seekers in the first place.[134]

The Refugee Convention only requires states to hear an asylum claim if a would-be refugee arrives at their border. States therefore employ a whole raft of measures in order to prevent asylum claims being lodged. In 2012, for instance, Canada spent money on a marketing campaign in Hungary aimed at discouraging Roma asylum seekers, warning they would be turned back should they try to claim asylum.[135] Other policies are more dramatic. In May 2013, Australia announced it would 'excise' the mainland from its migration zone, transferring asylum seekers who arrived by boat to detention centres on the tiny islands of Nauru, Manus and Christmas Island.[136]

Such policies *are* effective. In the UK, numbers of asylum seekers lodging claims fell rapidly after 2002, allowing then-Prime Minister Tony Blair to argue in the 2005 General Election campaign that 'it is precisely because we have been working hard at it that, over the past few years, asylum claims have fallen in Britain faster than anywhere else in Europe'.[137] More recent deterrence policies adopted in Canada have had similar dramatic success, halving the number of claims received in a single year, from 20,000 to 10,000.[138] But effective does not mean just. The risk is that these dramatic 'improvements' in asylum numbers reflect not just the rooting out of fraudsters but the locking out of 'real' refugees. Far from preserving the equity of asylum – far from underpinning the humanitarian exception to market migration – such policies remove the ability of the poor and the persecuted to seek vital protection.

The conviction that governments need to be 'tough on asylum' is similarly reflected in the fact that most asylum seekers in Britain do not become refugees. In the UK, decisions were made on nearly 17,000 asylum claims in 2012. Just over 6000 applicants were granted asylum or some other form of leave after an initial hearing. But a quarter of the negative decisions are later reversed on appeal. This means that a significant number of those initially stigmatised as 'failed' asylum seekers are later found to have a well-founded fear of persecution. In 2012, over half – 52% – of Syrians who were refused asylum at their first hearing were later granted refugee status on appeal, while 41% of Sri Lankan and 34% of Iranian 'failed' asylum seekers were also later found to be genuine refugees.[139]

The line between 'real' refugee and 'bogus' asylum seeker is thus often a mirage: but its real-life consequences can be devastating. No one knows this better than Deborah Kaymebe.[140] Today, Deborah's story is the stuff of inspiration: a former human rights barrister in the Congo, she has made a new life for herself and her two children in Scotland – learning English, working as a interpreter, writing a novel and becoming a British citizen in 2014. But when she arrived in the UK in 2005, eight months pregnant, her asylum claim was refused – twice. She later discovered this was largely because the translator had failed to recount her story accurately, causing the judge to doubt her credibility. Deborah spent the next two years caring for two small children while living on £81 a week: 'There is no future, you just live in fear. You think maybe I am going to lose everything'. It was not until 2007 that Deborah was able to make a third – finally successful – claim for asylum.[141]

Deborah's case is not unusual. In October 2013, the UK Parliament's Home Affairs Select Committee released a damning report describing the UK's asylum system as 'overburdened and under severe pressure'.[142] Bureaucratic delays mean that asylum claimants are required to live with uncertain status for years – in at least one case, *sixteen* years. Describing a culture of disbelief within the UK Border Agency, poor-quality decision making and 'general ineffectiveness', the Committee was clear: 'Ministers must not allow people who claim to be fleeing persecution to be left in limbo for so long ever again'.[143]

Asylum seekers stuck in purgatory speak above all of the anxieties that come from everyday poverty. For in the UK – like most other Western states – asylum seekers are not allowed to work. Instead, they must subsist on with minimal financial aid: single adult asylum seekers receive just £36.62 a week – 65% of the (reduced) rate paid to under-25s receiving income support. Poverty campaigners frequently underline how difficult it is for British families to survive on post-austerity benefits: asylum seekers are worse off still.[144] Could you live well – even adequately – on £36.62 a week: £5.23 a day?

As researchers have shown, the deprivation suffered by asylum seekers is not an unfortunate, unintended consequence: it is integral to the system. Intended to protect equal access to basic human rights, asylum policies in the West now entrench inequality. Poverty is a 'planned outcome of public [asylum] policy': it is intended to act as a deterrent to arrivals, and encourage others to leave voluntarily.[145] Tabloids may portray asylum seeker as 'benefit scroungers', duly castigated for relying upon hand-outs, but asylum seekers have no option *but* to accept state support: they are not allowed to work.[146]

Those who are refused refugee status are expected to go 'home'. Just over 10,000 failed asylum seekers were removed from the UK last year, the majority choosing to leave 'voluntarily' before they are forced to do so and while they are still eligible for assisted reintegration, including in some cases cash grants. But others fight their removal, fearing arrest, torture and death if they return. Such concerns are not unfounded. In February 2014, evidence obtained by *The Observer* suggested that the Congolese Interior Ministry has circulated papers sanctioning the torture 'with discretion' of government opponents, particularly those who were being 'refouled'[iv] by Western states.[147]

Other failed asylum seekers drop out of sight altogether, living like ghosts in order to avoid forced removal.[148] Those judged to be at 'high risk' of absconding are often detained, for as we saw in Chapter 5, there are considerable profits to be made detaining migrants – and in the UK asylum seekers can be detained indefinitely. In the year ending March 2013, 28,735 people entered a detention centre, and a similar number left, the majority asylum seekers. An average of 3000 were held at any one time. Despite Liberal Democrat leader Nick Clegg's pledge on entering government in May 2010 to end the practice of detaining children under immigration powers within a year, at least 37 children

---

[iv] Protection against *refoulement*, or forcible return, is a fundamental cornerstone of international refugee protection. Article 33 of the 1951 *Refugee Convention* states that 'No Contracting State shall expel or return ("refouler") a refugee in any manner whatsoever to the frontiers of territories where his life or freedom would be threatened'

were detained under the Immigration Act in the first three months of 2013.[149]

However, not all failed asylum seekers in detention centres are actually removed from the UK. Their state of origin may refuse to recognise their citizenship; they may be at risk of torture or an unfair trial upon return; they may be ill or pregnant, so not medically fit for deportation. Or their country may be considered too dangerous for them to be returned to, even if they don't personally qualify for refugee status. These failed asylum seekers who are awaiting removal – but who cannot actually be removed – are trapped. They are eligible only for a still further limited support – just £35.39 a week. This has to be loaded onto a pre-paid card, cannot be saved up to pay in bulk, and must be spent in designated shops, meaning that recipients cannot buy food in markets or pay bus fares. The British Red Cross estimates it assists 6,000 destitute asylum seekers and refugees each year.[150]

Nevertheless, if we can continue to pretend that the 'real' refugees are elsewhere, languishing in camps, keeping asylum seekers out can begin to look like a humanitarian act – as can deliberately impoverishing those who do arrive. Australians advocating for tougher asylum laws have argued that 'it is unfair that people should be able to pay their way on a boat to literally jump the queue … It is unfair that people will die in refugee camps waiting for their application to be processed while others pay to get a head start'.

This is a seductive narrative: but it demands an extraordinary degree of confidence in both our generosity and our ability to sort the deserving from the undeserving. In fact, only one refugee out of every hundred will ever be resettled from a camp to a third country in the West. Some resettlement programmes are so small as to be largely symbolic: Japan, for instance, has taken in just 90 refugees over three years as part of a resettlement pilot programme. The UK only began to resettle refugees in 2003, and currently takes 750 a year. In February 2014, the UK government undertook to provide a further 500 resettlement places for the 'most vulnerable' victims of the Syrian refugee crisis, but by July had resettled just 50.[151]

Of course, just as in any lottery, some refugees do win the resettlement prize. In 2012, 69,252 refugees were resettled, the overwhelming majority – over 75% – to the US. But privileging extreme vulnerability among desperate people can have unintended consequences, creating a new political economy around 'proving' need. Resettlement can be corrupted, too, especially when ten million refugees are vying for a place on the waiting list. In some camps refugees are able to buy their way onto the resettlement list, purchasing an already-approved file or persuading officials to sanction a family 'reunion' with a wife or sister they have never met.[152]

When it comes to immigration, asylum is supposed to be the safety net: the sanctuary that means that, even if borders preserve inequality, they are not inhumane. And although we might prefer to think that most asylum seekers are fraudulent, the truth is that it is abundantly clear that there are millions of poor, persecuted and defeated souls trapped in hellholes beyond our borders, living miserable lives. There are plenty of 'real refugees'. The real question is whether we have the obligation to *do* anything about it. Basic principles of social justice suggest that at the very least, we should not deliberately seek to deter those asylum seekers who try to make the journey here, and that we should not condemn those who do arrive to long years of structural poverty. Our lifeboats are not full, and we should not allow immigration hysteria to poison humanitarian commitments.

We would also do well to heed history's lessons. In the 1930s, asylum policies were similarly determined by immigration politics. A 1938 poll, for instance, showed that while 94% of Americans disapproved of *Kristallnacht*, 77% believed the US should not raise quotas to permit additional Jewish migration. Even existing US quotas were not filled during the 1930s, due to policies excluding all those 'likely to become a public charge'.[153] The persecuted were simply too poor to be admitted. In Britain, UK parliamentarians were similarly emphatic that population density and a crowded Britain meant that 'it is impossible for us to absorb any large number of refugees here'.[154] We know the end of that sorry tale now: so right and wrong are obvious. The refusal of states to admit refugee-migrants led directly to internment and death.[155] Who would send Jews back to Germany in 1939? Who wouldn't rather their great-grandfather prove to be a people smuggler, as opposed to an immigration officer, in 1940s Europe? Today, asylum seekers are similarly stigmatised – 'poor', 'devious', 'liars' – because public anxieties about immigration have driven most Western governments to work to shut out as many poor as possible.

Yet it is equally important to recognise that the distortions that fed that taxi driver's instinctive reaction to the migrants crossing the street do reflect genuine and deep anxieties about what poor migrants mean for the West's own working classes. Just like in the 1930s, in reality we balance our commitment to global justice against very personal and immediate social and economic fears. So even if our attitudes to asylum are shameful, when it comes to the broader, interlinked questions about *immigration* and inequality, we do need to pay close attention to local worries. It's time to answer the question: do migrants take our jobs?

8 FOR RICHER, FOR POORER

Immigration is not just compatible with, but a necessary component of economic growth.
Dave Reichert, US Congressman (Republican), 2008

When it comes to talking about immigration and inequality, what most people *really* want to know is whether immigration makes us poorer. The difficulty in answering that question lies not so much in the economics as determining who 'we' are. For there is pretty conclusive evidence that – in macroeconomic terms – immigration fosters economic growth. The UK Treasury estimates that immigration was responsible for around 15–20% of total economic growth in the UK from 2001–6.[156] In 2008 the Trades Union Congress (TUC) concurred, concluding that 'overall, immigration has been good for this country ... we have more jobs, higher wages, better services and lower taxes than we would have had without immigration'.[157]

These figures underline that immigration clearly contributes to overall economic wealth. But they say little about *who* gains other than migrants themselves (as we saw in Chapter 3). Do ordinary Britons and Americans profit from migration? Or do migrants' gains come at the expense of other workers – so that, although there's more money in the economy, working-class nationals have less of it, while elites profit? In other words, is immigration good for growth – but bad for national inequality?

In 2012, the Government's Migration Advisory Committee (MAC) considered the question of exactly whose welfare should be considered when assessing the economic impacts of immigration. MAC's preference was to focus on trying to ascertain the economic impact of immigration on 'residents', setting to one side the larger gains that migrants make through migrating.[158]

In national terms, this might make political sense, but if we're interested in measuring global inequality, discarding the gains migrants make is counterintuitive. As development economists Michael Clemens and Lance Pritchett have pointed out, 'while production has a place, people, not patches of earth, have wellbeing'. Measuring migration through only the effect on citizens who are resident in their *own* country effectively erases the economic contributions of both immigrants and emigrants. Clemens and Pritchett have argued that what we should really measure is 'income-per-natural' – the wealth of all of a country's citizens regardless of where they live. This would help to ensure that the link between migration and development is not forgotten. As we saw in Chapter 3, in global terms migration certainly helps to combat inequality.[159]

But what about inequality here, within our own communities? One way of measuring the impact of immigration on inequality in the West is to look at the relationship between job creation and immigration. Between 1997 and 2014, an extra 3.2 million jobs were added to the UK economy. Thirty million people are now employed in the UK (there were 26.2 million employed in 1997). The number of non-UK nationals working in the UK grew rapidly in the same time period – from 928,000 foreign workers in January 1997 to 2.7 million by December 2013.[160]

It's easy to read these figures and conclude that migrants must have taken a large number of these new jobs. Add to this the fact that unemployment stands at around 2.5 million, and it's simple to put two and two together and make five: 'Migration *IS* killing off jobs'.[161] Yet this is statistical sleight-of-hand, ignoring the intangible effect of the role a growing population plays in creating new jobs for themselves. The Oxford Migration Observatory offers a less dramatic – but more accurate – assessment of how immigration affects the labour market: 'migrants account for 16% of newly hired people, but we're not sure if they're doing newly created jobs or not, and we don't know whether those jobs would exist if the migrants weren't here'.[162]

Thinking in these terms busts wide open what's often called the 'lump of labour' fallacy: the idea that there are a fixed number of jobs in the economy, so that any job taken by an immigrant *must* displace a national worker. When immigrants arrive, they don't just fill jobs in the existing economy. They are consumers too: they buy food, and clothes, and bus tickets, and send their children to schools. To meet these demands, existing businesses expand and new businesses are created. There is also a long association between migration and entrepreneurship. From Patek's Mango Chutney in the UK, to Mi Pueblo Food's tortillas in the US, there is a long list of multi-million dollar businesses that were created to meet distinctly new, immigrant-fuelled demands.

We know, however, that migrants are not a homogenous group, and that they arrive with very different sets of skills, intentions and expectations. One alternative to the deregulated free movement that occurs in the EU is a much more tightly controlled system, in which national governments work to attract the 'best' migrants.

Across the West, there's an assumption the 'best' immigrants are those who come armed with Master's degrees, preferably in the 'STEM' subjects that Western students are increasingly reluctant to specialise in – Science, Technology, Engineering and Mathematics. Setting high bars to migration ensures that these 'desirable' migrants can fill skill gaps, but the poor are kept out. As a result, many highly skilled and highly paid workers already enjoy extensive freedom of movement. The UK, for instance, already exempts jobs that pay a salary of £150,000 or more from its skilled migrant quotas. PhD level jobs in the UK are also exempt from its resident labour market tests, so that 'employers may recruit the most suitable person for the job, not necessarily the most suitable person from the resident labour force'.[163]

This is largely uncontroversial. Few would argue that the City's well-heeled bankers deserve protection – especially given it's the global principles of free trade and deregulation that make them rich. The appointment of Canadian Mark Carney to run the Bank of England is not because there was no British citizen who *could* do the job, but because he was considered the *best* candidate. Our political parties follow this practice too: the British general election in 2015 will be a battle between an Australian and an American political strategist, fighting to win over British voters.

Similarly, despite intermittent calls for quotas to be reintroduced into Premiership football in order to nurture home-grown talent, any expectations that this would raise standards assume – bizarrely – that *protection* from competition breeds success. As Manchester United manager Sir Alex Ferguson wrote in 2008, 'I did not start the final of the Uefa Champions League with six Englishmen because I was making a political statement. I did it because they're good enough to win the European Cup'.[164]

It's hard to argue that high-skilled workers really need nationalist protections against high-skilled immigrants at all. The real question is where the line between this high-skilled free market and the rest of the labour force should be drawn. Exactly where 'fair' lies is a question of politics, but – given the existing exemption of highly paid and PhD-level jobs from such tests – it seems that we have already accepted that the line lies *somewhere*. Nevertheless, in recent years there has been a general trend to tie visas for highly skilled foreign workers to named employers. Ostensibly, this helps protect local workers from an influx of highly qualified but jobless migrants. In practice, however, it gives sponsoring employers real power at the expense of the 'best' migrants. Nowhere is this more evident than in the US.

At first glance, it's hard to believe that Sunnyvale, California, is the beating heart of the modern American Dream. Six lanes of traffic cut through a concrete jungle of strip malls and neon lights. Yet it's in Sunnyvale that one very twenty-first century American Dream is unfolding. Next to the Vietnamese *pho* café – a reminder of migrations past – a huge crowd of Indians queue to order *dosas* at the Madras Cafe. These are Silicon Valley's engineers: well-paid, well-educated Indians who are powering the booming 'American' hi-tech economy.

Most – though not all – of these Indian software engineers are in the US on H-1B visas, 65,000 of which are issued every year – with an additional 20,000 available for those who hold an advanced degree from a US university. But applying for an H-1B is a cumbersome, bureaucratic process, in part because demand for H-1B visas hugely outstrips limited supply. The US Immigration service opens the annual application process for H-1Bs on 1 April, for entry the next financial year. In 2013, the '2014 H-1B Cap Season' was closed five days later: 124,000 applications had been received. Costs of filing an H1-B petition can easily run to five figures. The result of a legal and financial arms race is that it is increasingly only big companies that can afford to play H1-B roulette – and they, too, lose far more often then they'd like.[165]

Hi-tech companies have repeatedly lobbied for more high-skilled tech visas to be made available. In this campaign, much has been made of the fact that Silicon Valley's global dominance of the software industry rests upon the shoulders of immigrants. Between 2006 and 2012, a quarter of companies founded in American had at least one foreign-born founder: that figure rose to 44% in Silicon Valley. Those companies were responsible for employing 560,000 workers, and bringing in $63 billion in sales. Yahoo, eBay, Intel, Google all had at least one immigrant co-founder.[166]

Yet pointing to the staggering innovation of Silicon Valley to make the case for more H-1B migrants – rather than wholesale immigration reform – is disingenuous. Many of those who are lauded as 'immigrant' co-founders are not labour migrants. To take just one example, Sergey Brin – co-founder of Google – arrived as a child with his parents from Soviet Russia. In fact, H-1B visas are not well placed to facilitate innovation or job creation. This is because H-1B workers are supposed to be 'shortage' workers: so their permission to stay is conditional upon continuing to work for their sponsoring employers. Couple that with the US fire-at-will labour laws, and it's clear that even if H-1B workers are highly skilled, they are also indentured labourers.

H-1B visas distort the balance of power between workers and employers. In order to move *into* the American labour market, H-1B visa holders have to give up their freedom to move *within* the labour market after they arrive. H-1B visas are also furiously opposed by many American workers – who argue that, far from filling shortages, H-1Bs simply allow big business to exploit American workers, driving down pay and replacing experienced native labourers with foreigners that Americans are expected to train up before they themselves are fired.[167]

In the event, research from the Brookings Institute suggests that H-1Bs are not, in fact, driving down wages: H1-B visa holders earn *more* – not less – than equivalent US workers even when the data is broken down by age, occupation and educational qualification.[168] Companies don't pay more in order to endure the hassle and uncertainty (as well as the additional expense) of importing foreign labour unless it's really necessary. But what *is* true is that by tying employees to employers, H-1Bs reduce the bargaining power of the migrant workers. Such migrants may be reluctant to speak up and question management decisions, making them more 'desirable' employees than their American counterparts. By allowing capital to set the terms of immigration, H-1B visas may well compound structural inequality. Yet these negative effects could be best tempered by *opening up* the labour market, thus allowing H-1B visa holders the freedom to move between jobs once they arrive in America and redistributing power away from employers.

However, while it may sound appealing to imagine Western economies competing for the 'brightest and best', the OECD has warned that 'there is no guarantee under supply-driven systems that high-skilled migrants will work in high-skilled occupations'. In the UK there's evidence that half of skilled migrants currently work in unskilled jobs: Denmark's 'Green Card' scheme found the same problem of over-qualification, as those admitted as graduates failed to find graduate-level work.[169] So should we really put a premium on a degree when what we need are plumbers and taxi drivers? Such an elite-driven approach to labour migration ignores the gaps at the bottom: not the jobs that Britons and Americans *can't* do, but the jobs they *won't* do.

But are there *really* jobs that the indigenous workforce won't do? Or are migrants just stealing jobs, undercutting Western workers who can't afford to feed their families on lower wages? Rates of immigration appear to have very little effect on whether citizens are in work or not.[170] This is partly because economic migration is often circular, seasonal and temporary. When the work dries up, such migrants usually will go back home, or move on to the next town or country where work *is* available. There is, however, some evidence to suggest that under certain circumstances – particularly in times of recession – some native workers with few qualifications do lose out. In 2012, the UK Migration Advisory Committee published research suggesting that, in times of economic depression, there *was* an association between the employment of recently arrived non-EU migrants and the displacement of some lower-skilled native workers. Between 1995 and 2010, for every 100 non-EU recently arrived migrant workers employed who had arrived in the past five years, it appeared that 23 Britons lost their jobs. Overall, for every 13 new 'migrant' jobs that were created during this period, one 'British' job was 'lost'.[171]

The anti-immigrant lobby seized on the study as proof of the harm that immigration wreaks. But in fact, the findings were extremely tentative. A follow-up report stressed that the link seems to be statistically significant *only* in periods of recession, and *only* when looking at recently arrived *non-EU* migrants. This may be because when the economy is growing, new migrants fill new jobs. When the economy is shrinking, there are fewer newer jobs for new migrants to fill – which means more migrants compete directly with citizen workers for the jobs that remain. The ability of *European* migrants to move freely across the continent means these migrants are 'more likely to return home if the economic prospects in the UK deteriorate', so don't 'take' British jobs at all.[172] Other non-EU migrants know that once they leave, they may struggle to return. The resulting job squeeze may therefore be a consequence not of migration laws that are too lax, but migration laws that are too restrictive.

Of course, it's not just about whether jobs exist. It's also about the conditions and pay attached. Decent work demands decent wages. If migration pulls wages down, businesses and consumers benefit: but workers will suffer. In the UK, studies suggest the effects of immigration on wages are fairly minimal. This is probably because national minimum wage legislation provides a floor: an ethical limit imposed upon the competitive drive of the market. In 2012, the Migration Advisory Committee concluded that in overall terms, the effect of immigration on wages in the UK is negligible. As a result of 2.1 million additional migrant workers arriving in Britain between 1995 and 2010, workers' wages may have dropped by £1.15 a day – or increased by the same marginal amount.[173]

When these figures are broken down by income and skill level, however, it becomes clear that once again it is the lowest-skilled and lowest-paid workers who are most likely to be losing out as a result of additional migrant labour arriving in the UK. One study suggests the lowest 10% of earners lost £1 a year for every extra 10,000 migrants; another that semi-skilled and unskilled workers lost £8. Yet average and high-paid workers tended to earn more as more migrants arrived – £4 and £5 per year per 10,000 additional migrants respectively. Skilled professionals made a £15 gain. While the numbers involved here are relatively small, they strongly suggest that migration can exacerbate inequalities within our existing communities, and that the benefits and burdens of migration are not shared equally among the local workforce.[174]

In the US, Harvard Professor George Borjas is famous for making a similar argument. Looking at the impact of Mexican immigration between 1980 and 2000, Borjas' models suggest that although educated Americans did not lose out because of immigration, US high-school dropouts suffered a 8.2% fall in wages in the short term, and a 5% loss in the long-term, as a result of competition with low-skilled Mexican migrants.[175] Yet it's important to note that Borjas' work has been subject to fierce criticism from other economists, notably Berkeley economist David Card. Card's research suggests that ultimately, the effect of immigration on wage inequality is very small: that in the US, immigration is responsible for only 4-6% of the rise in domestic income inequality since the 1980s.[176] Other political and social structures are far more important in perpetuating inequality.

One way to start addressing the impact of migration upon the low-paid would thus be to enforce existing employment laws that are intended to provide a minimum floor to the labour market. The fruits of our collective-bargaining powers – minimum wages, health and safety laws – are after all the laws that help to limit the power of capital, and keep workers safe. The low wages and long hours that irregular immigrants may be prepared to work or are forced to work – in breach of these laws – are therefore triply harmful. Citizen workers may lose their jobs as businesses employ cheaper undocumented staff; irregular immigrants may be forced to work in unsafe and exploitative conditions; and society as a whole is left diminished, in thrall to avaricious capital.

Irregular immigrants are particularly vulnerable. Without papers, it's difficult to demand that your employer follow the EU Working Time Directive. There is a wealth of research detailing the often gruelling and occasionally appalling conditions faced by irregular workers – from the withholding of wages already earned to sexual abuse. If such work is cash-in-hand, society suffers a further blow: social security and taxes will not be paid, depriving the community of resources. Yet when it comes to exploiting low-paid workers, many more of us are complicit than we'd care to admit, enmeshed in a low-wage market economy. We're not just consumers of fast-food burgers and clothes that are made in China: we employ women from Mexico or Romania or Vietnam in our own homes.

In February 2014, the UK Minister for Immigration was forced to resign, after it emerged that he had –

unknowingly – employed an undocumented cleaner, who was later deported. He was not the first British minister to resign for breaking his own immigration rules. In 2009, the UK Attorney General was fined £5000 for – unwittingly – employing an irregular migrant as a housekeeper, who was later placed in detention.[177] Irregular migrants often live in the shadows; but they often do so while servicing the demands of Western middle-class professionals for clean streets, clean toilets and clean houses.[178] Irregular migration undoubtedly perpetuates inequality: workers fearful of deportation don't join unions.

So far, we've focused on the ways in which migration may make it harder for low-skilled indigenous cohorts to find work. But what if in fact, immigration helps mask the fact that many long-term unemployed *won't* work? Despite high levels of migration in the past decade, rates of economic inactivity among the British working-age population have remained relatively stable since the 1970s, at around 20%.[179]

Questioning why these citizens aren't working involves making judgments not just about the workers, but also about the work itself. Ultimately, immigration here is a sideshow: this is a debate about an entire economic system, and the balance it strikes between growth and equity. As researchers have pointed out, if health care assistants' wages were raised above the minimum wage, more British workers would certainly do the job. But home-care pay rates in the UK are heavily influenced by what local councils are willing to pay – because they buy in 80% of home-care help. These local councils are also facing billion-pound funding gaps as a result of cuts in central government grants. To fund better-paid home care for the elderly, disabled and ill first requires us to accept higher tax rates.[180] One result of such reforms would be fewer migrant and more British health-care workers. But for now, it's not migration that keeps wages low and makes the jobs unpalatable for native workers. It's the logic of capitalism, accompanied by a cut-price social contract.

Furthermore, when it comes to some categories of low-skilled labour, citizen-workers are a very poor substitute for migrants. Many of us are overqualified. We're less mobile than migrants: we're reluctant to leave our homes, our family and our friends behind to take up work in another town or part of the country, especially if that work is seasonal or temporary. Traditionally, the heavy physical labour involved in construction or farm work has always attracted a highly mobile workforce of fit, strong and unattached males from rural populations. Irish labourers, for instance, played a crucial role in building Britain's canals and railways in the nineteenth century.[181]

In particular, Western countries have a serious shortage of farm labourers. Though the details vary, most developed states run special programmes admitting a specified quota of farm labourers – often from specific source countries – for a limited period, setting out strict conditions for employment, including minimum wage levels. In the UK, a Seasonal Agricultural Workers' Scheme (SAWS) was in place for sixty years, though after 2007 it was only open to workers from Romania and Bulgaria. In 2014, when workers from these states gained full and free access to the EU labour markets, SAWS came to an end. Despite the Migration Advisory Committee's conclusions that the scheme was 'extremely well managed, that 'most parties gain', and that 'British workers are not displaced by SAWS', there is no plan to develop a replacement programme. The results, British farmers fear, could be catastrophic: 95% believe their business will suffer, as they can't find the workers to harvest their crops.[182] One farmer reported that having tried to recruit 14 local English people for seasonal work, the average stay – for those working outside during the harvest – was just 5 days. The Romanian and Bulgarian workers, in contrast, were described as 'very intelligent … willing to work … we assume that only the best come here, because it must take a lot of drive to leave home and go to a foreign country to seek work'.[183]

The UK government currently argues that there's no need for another SAWS, because Romanian and Bulgarian workers will still be available to work in the fields, without needing any special permission to do so. However this ignores one crucial fact about agricultural work: it's not just Western Europeans who don't want to work in the fields. Eastern Europeans aren't so keen to do so either. If they can work in other sectors – less physically demanding, more interesting, more sociable – they will. When Poland joined the EU in 2004, and its citizens gained the right to work in Britain, the numbers working on farms dropped, as they looked for less seasonal work closer to towns and which better reflected their education and qualifications.[184]

To harvest their fields, it appears that farmers don't just need any migrant workers: they need *tied* migrant workers. The UK Migration Advisory committee was right to say that a 'replacement SAWS would mean horticulture is treated as a favoured sector', winning exemption from the rules that prohibit other sectors recruiting low-skilled workers from outside the EU. But there is surely an irony in recognising that such 'favour' would involves granting access to a *wider* labour market.[185]

It's the very opposite of the monopolies that fans of free markets normally condemn.

There are some alternatives to shipping in seasonal migrants to tend our crops. But it is questionable whether we are prepared to live with the consequences of making such decisions. Accelerated technological adaptation could replace some workers: but this would mean England's green and pleasant land being more rapidly and more extensively covered with plastic poly-tunnels. The greatest irony of all is that the apple orchards and the hop-fields that for many people *are* the 'England' they're terrified of losing to immigration can only continue to flourish thanks to migrant labour. British food for British families: it's brought to your table by Bulgarians.

So what effect *does* immigration have on economic inequality? At a global scale, migration clearly works to redress long-standing inequity. But at a local level, we live in a world where privilege has grossly distorted the power of capital to exploit labour, and in which the poor compete – and are sometimes harmed – by cheap migrant labour. There are already subsidies and taxes that we accept we should pay in order to share growth and opportunity and maintain social cohesion. Placing some restrictions on the free movement of unskilled labour – to protect those citizens that Western states have failed to equip and train for the twenty-first-century labour market – is at least temporarily justified. Yet such protections would be far more effective – and on a far less discriminatory basis – if the limits placed on the market were not a fence at the border, but effective enforcement of existing legislation supposed to protect all workers – whether migrant or citizen. Low-wage immigration is in part a reflection of broader societal inequalities and the failure to adequately police exploitation. In one recent report on low-skilled immigration, for example, MAC pointed out that 'a firm can expect a visit from HMRC inspectors once in every 250 years and expect to be prosecuted once in a million years. Such enforcement effort hardly provides an incentive to abide by the national minimum wages'.[186] So when it comes to talking about inequality and immigration, what we may really be talking about is ensuring decent work for decent wages. You don't need to build such tall walls in order to achieve this if you first built a floor.

9 FROM CRADLE TO GRAVE

Social rights imply an absolute right to a certain standard of civilisation ... their content does not depend on the economic value of the individual claimant.
    T.H. Marshall, *Citizenship and Social Class,* 1950

Immigrants, however, are not just workers: they are also human beings. They get ill; they have children; they live in local communities. And there is a widespread belief that, in the words of Immigration Minister Damien Green, 'unlimited migration has placed unacceptable pressure on our public services'.[187] Some of this is clearly pure invention: claims that UK pensioners receive only £6000 a year while asylum seekers are given £29,000 are just lies.[188] But many scholars *have* suggested that having a strong welfare state makes it harder for a community to welcome immigrants.[189]

Schools and hospitals are the bricks and mortar that make a nation-state's commitment to equal citizenship real. Every Western state has some form of welfare state that insures the sick, feeds the poor, and educates the next generation of taxpayers. The details vary from state to state, but even in the US – usually presented as having the loosest of social safety nets – programmes like Medicare, Social Security and Food Stamps still account for 58% of federal tax spending.[190] But it is not clear how immigrants fit into this model. Should they qualify for benefits as taxpayers – or be excluded as non-citizens? Does immigration undermine already-creaking public services – and in doing so perpetuate local inequality?

In fact, as an international migrant, the chances are that your social rights are already severely limited, at the very least until you become a permanent resident. Most migrants arriving in the UK from places outside the EU will have 'no recourse to public funds' stamped in their passport.[191] These immigrants have no right to apply for housing benefit, income support, child tax credits or income-based job seekers' allowance (JSA).[192] As an L2 visa holder in the US, I have no recourse to public assistance – and won't do until five years after I get my green card.[193] Nevertheless, the belief that migrants overload public services and take advantage of generous Western benefit systems is pervasive, especially because intra-EU migrants *do* qualify for some benefits as EU citizens.

However 'benefits tourists' are easier to imagine in theory than to spot in practice. In October 2013, the EU released *A Fact-finding Analysis on the Member States' Social Security Systems of the entitlements of non-active intra-EU migrants to special non-contributory cash benefits and healthcare granted on the basis of residence*.[194] What the report lacked in terms of headline appeal, it made up for in empirical evidence. The findings were conclusive. Non-active EU migrants are a tiny proportion of the population across Europe – 0.7% to 1% of the total EU population. In the

UK, where 4% of the population are EU migrants, just 1.2% of the total population are economically 'non-active' EU migrants. This label encompasses pensioners, homemakers and parents as well as unemployed job seekers. In the UK, 1 in 4 of these 'non-active' EU migrants are full-time students – who are paying fees to study here, and who are extremely unlikely to be claiming benefits.[195]

None of this adds up to a benefits-tourism 'crisis', particularly not in the UK – which, as the report points out, is the only EU country in which fewer EU citizens claim unemployment benefit than nationals (1% as opposed to 4%). Furthermore, of 1.44 million claiming job seekers' allowance in 2011, only 8.5% were non-UK nationals, and only a quarter of these – 38,000 claimants – were from the EU.[196] Furthermore, evidence from the British Department of Work and Pensions shows that the habitual residence tests already weed out many claims made by Eastern European migrants. In 2011, two-thirds of claims by A8 migrants for income-related benefits were refused.[197] This, at the very least, would seem to suggest that existing rules are already managing to protect our benefits systems from nefarious interlopers.

The vast majority of EU migrants pay into the collective system without taking out. In 2009, a UCL study led by Christian Dustmann found that – on comparing net tax receipts with likely expenditure – Eastern European A8 migrants paid in 35% more than they were likely to receive in welfare services, while natives' taxes were equivalent to only 80% of the money they received in benefits. Although different models of income and outgoings shifted the balance slightly in local citizens' favour, Dustmann's conclusions were clear: 'A8 immigrants are unambiguously net fiscal contributors, while natives are unambiguously receiving more than they contribute'.[198] It is migrants, not natives, who give back to the welfare state far more than they take: migration doesn't undermine as much as underpin the fiscal sustainability of our social safety nets.

These findings have been backed up by other economists' work, which have similarly suggested that 'the relative balance between what they cost and what they contribute is firmly weighted towards a very substantial contribution'.[199] The evidence to support a crackdown on benefits tourism looks shaky. If we measure legitimate access to the welfare system and public services in terms of financial contribution, it's hard to justify any long-term restrictions on migrants' access to benefits in their host country. As Polish foreign minister Radek Sikorski asked in response to UK Prime Minister David Cameron's strong rhetoric on welfare and migration in 2013, 'if Britain gets our taxpayers, shouldn't it also pay their benefits?'.[200]

But what about irregular migrants? The government cannot trace or tax cash-in-hand transactions, and certainly, many irregular migrants are happy to remain in the shadow economy. However, irregular immigrants *do* pay some tax. In the US, it is estimated that irregular migrants paid the US Treasury at least $10.6 billion in 2010 alone, including payroll taxes. As a result, in April 2013 government actuaries concluded that 'the presence of unauthorized workers in the United States has, on average, *a positive effect* on the financial status of the Social Security programme'.[201] The same is likely to be true in the UK. Tabloid headlines may scream that '600 000 illegals are given National Insurance numbers', but by obtaining NI numbers, these irregular migrants are also making fiscal contributions they are unlikely to ever benefit from personally.[202]

Of course, understanding what more migrants may mean for our public services isn't purely a question of counting pennies and restricting benefit payments. We also need to think about how migrants *use* public services like hospitals and schools – and how this may impact inequality within our communities.

In the UK, commitment to the provision of universal health care through the National Health Service has resulted in particular concerns about immigrants misusing the service. In early 2013, UK Health Secretary Jeremy Hunt vowed to combat an 'epidemic of health tourism' with a host of new proposals, including an annual health-care levy of £200 for all UK-bound migrants (except those with private insurance) who are not permanent residents.[203] On inspection, however, 'health tourism' is no more pervasive than 'benefits tourism'. The total amount spent on migrant health care is probably somewhere in the region of £2 billion: but this figure includes the £1.76 billion cost of providing health care for migrants who have been living – and so working and paying taxes – for up to five years. Costs for deliberate abuse, and what the report labels incremental 'advantage-taking' after arrival (where migrants and visitors access the NHS legally, but more frequently than they would do should they have to pay) – are more likely to come to between £110 and £280 million. This is still a significant sum, but it is worth remembering that the cost of the NHS in England is £100 billion. Even assuming the upper-bound estimate is right, such 'health tourism' takes up just 0.28% of the total NHS budget.[204]

In fact, migrants cost the NHS less per head than do citizens. In 2012, the overall cost per head for NHS services in England was estimated at £1726. Yet once we adjust for age and gender profiles, the average annual cost of migrants using the NHS is just £1004. This figure still overestimates migrant use of the NHS: studies have show that migrants in the UK consistently appear to report *better health* than their UK counterparts. Once you add that factor in, the cost per head of providing NHS services to migrants falls to £866 per head per year.[205]

Other forms of 'health tourism', however, are being actively encouraged. Figures suggest that medical tourism generated £219 million in extra spending in 2011 – 50% from wealthy Middle Eastern visitors. Research by the London School of Hygiene and Tropical Medicine and the University of York found that eighteen hospitals were making at least £42 million through treatment of foreign patients. In a further twist, it appears that Britons are more likely to seek medical treatment elsewhere – often for fertility treatments, cosmetic surgery or bariatric surgery with long waiting lists in the UK – than foreigners are to travel to the UK in search of medical treatment.[206]

All this suggests that angst about deliberately fraudulent health tourism seems misplaced: there is no evidence of widespread misuse. Yet these discussions – particularly the expansion of luxury 'health tourism' alongside the introduction of a migrant health care levy in the UK – *do* reflect a wider dispute about the status of health care as a social right. The uneasy co-existence of a growing for-profit market in health care – welcoming only those that can pay – with the social provision of universally accessible health care, hints at the extent to which debates about migrants and the NHS are part of a wider debate about welfare entitlements and growing social inequality. Legal migrants are now being asked to pay a £200 deposit upfront because they have not yet contributed enough through taxation to qualify for free-at-the-point-of-access NHS care. In the future, citizens' access to health care might also depend upon showing a receipt.

It's also important to remember that the NHS – and the provision of equal access to health care for all residents – runs on migrant labour. Ever since its foundation in 1948, NHS has relied upon foreign health-care workers: the first Caribbean nurses arrived on the *Empire Windrush*. Even while unrolling plans for tight new restrictions on immigration in April 2011, UK Prime Minister David Cameron acknowledged that 'go into any hospital and you'll find people from Uganda, India and Pakistan who are caring for our sick and vulnerable'.[207]

Reliance upon overseas medical staff has continued. Today, the General Medical Council estimates that 37% of doctors in the UK qualified overseas – 27% outside Europe. Yet there has been a marked drop in the number of young foreign doctors under 30 arriving in the UK because of new visa restrictions, and there are concerns about what this will mean for long-term staffing levels.[208] Britain is not alone in worrying about how to find enough doctors though. Nearly every health system in the developed world depends upon migrant labour. The UK bemoans the loss of its doctors to Australia, New Zealand and the US – while Romania complains that its doctors are leaving for Britain. In Australia, 56% of general doctors and 47% of specialists are born overseas, along with 33% of nurses.[209]

But the real health worker crises are in middle- and low-income states. The World Health Organisation (WHO) estimates that globally, there are a missing 7.2 million skilled health workers – and has argued that the problem is exacerbated by 'brain drain', as physicians and nurses from developing countries emigrate to the West, lured by higher salaries and better-functioning health systems.[210] Critics argue that it is equivalent to rich states 'stealing' from poor ones to plug their own training gaps, entrenching global health inequalities. Such worries have led to concerted efforts to regulate and reduce overseas medical recruitment, premised on the idea that less health-worker migration is better for poor countries.[211]

Yet such strategies are not necessarily good for poor *people*. Reducing the freedom of health workers to migrate subordinates individual choice to national interest: this is illiberal. Restricting individuals' equality of opportunity in the hope of preserving some equality of outcome is foolish. As Michael Clemens has pointed out, in many of the least-developed countries rural-urban imbalance is often as much of a problem as emigration – in Kenya, 66% of doctors are to be found in Nairobi, where just 8% of the population live. In fact, research suggests that, in some cases, prospects of emigration may not lead to brain drain but aid brain *gain*, as more students are trained. The Philippines, for instance, is the long-time leading exporter of nurses – but because it has invested in training, it also has more nurses per capita in-country than the UK.[212] The solution to the global health-care workers shortage is not to erect barriers, but to build medical schools – perhaps *especially* in developing countries, where the prospect of emigration is both a powerful incentive for individuals and a means of redressing global inequality through the movement of people from south to north. Rather than level down, we should aspire to build up.All this suggests that immigrants aren't bad for our health. But are they bad for our education? If educating immigrant children takes place at the expense of local children's learning then the effects of migration on schools may compound other disadvantages, leaving local children already suffering social deprivation still worse off.

There is near-universal consensus that by far the most serious impediment to academic achievement is poverty. This is part explains why so much of the academic literature has tended to focus on comparing the educational achievements of children from ethnic minorities – who tend by default to have a recent immigrant past – with those of poor white children. So how do these children do once they have arrived at school? A large number of poor migrant children – particularly from Chinese and Indian families – significantly outperform their white peers both in the UK and the US. Figures from Ofsted, for instance, show that in 2013 only 32% of white British students who are eligible for free school meals[v] achieved 5 'good' grades at GCSE, but 42% of Black Caribbean, 47% of Pakistani, 59% of Bangladeshi and 77% of Chinese students do.[213]

Research by sociologists Tomas Jiménez and Adam Horowitz in the US has similarly mapped how in the majority-minority state of California, the migration of high-skilled Asian families has shifted cultural expectations to the extent that immigration and achievement have become linked in new ways: 'Asianness is intimately associated with high achievement, hard work, and academic success' but 'whiteness... stands for lower achievement, laziness and mediocrity'. In the highly competitive schools of Cupertino, California, white students who study are "Asian at heart".[214]

---

[v] Children are eligible for free school meals if their parents or guardians are in receipt of income support benefits, making this a useful measure of relative socio-economic deprivation.

It has been argued that the effort of teaching difficult migrant schoolchildren – such as Latinos in the US and Afro-Caribbean boys in the UK, who often don't speak English when they arrive, or who face an uphill struggle to escape low cultural expectations and poverty – draws resources away from poor white children. But in fact there is evidence that, in the UK, the higher the number of pupils speaking English as an Additional Language in a school, the *higher* the level of achievement for *all* students, including those who speak only English. Although the reasons for this are not fully understood, researchers are clear: 'high levels of migration are not in general associated with worse school performance or poorer outcomes for non-migrant children: if anything, the reverse'.[215]

It's important to recognise, of course, that the relationship between poverty and migration doesn't only impact educational outcomes. The public are equally convinced, for instance, of links between poverty, migration and crime. But while the West may be in the midst of a migration wave, it is emphatically *not* in the midst of a crime wave. In the UK, crime rates have fallen continuously since 2002, a drop that coincided with Eastern European arrivals.[216] In the US, since 1990 there has been a 45% drop in violent crime, and a 42% drop in property crime. During the same period, the number of unauthorised migrants climbed from 3.5 million to 11 million, and the percentage of the population who were foreign born rose from 8% to 13%.[217] Correlation, of course, is not causation. But it is a good indication that more migration does not translate into more crime. Our streets have never been safer – although many of us have also never been more frightened.

This is the opposite of what we might expect. Social disorganisation theory links migration and crime: it suggests that as diversity increases, communities are destabilised, and this results in increased crime rates.[218] Yet more recent analyses show that the opposite is actually true. In the UK, immigrant 'enclaves' – defined as neighbourhoods where at least 30% of the neighbourhood are immigrants – have lower levels of crime and victimisation than similar socio-economic areas without a large immigrant presence.[219] Researchers from the US have similarly concluded that 'broad reductions in violent crime during recent years are partially attributable to *increases* in immigration'.[220]

Health care, an education and a home in a secure neighbourhood are among the most fundamental entitlements recognised in international law.[221] Yet, like all human rights, making them real comes with a price tag – and depends upon a promise of community solidarity. If realising our rights becomes dependent on being able to afford them financially as *individuals*, then they are no longer rights, just privileges. Equality of opportunity suffers, and national solidarity unravels.

Nevertheless, despite tabloid insinuation and public hostility, there is no evidence that migrants abuse the health system, or crowd out local pupils. In fact, migrant medics deliver our health care, and migrant pupils help raise achievement in schools. Diversity also seems to offer some protection against crime. The real enemy – whether measured in petty thefts, GCSE grades or life expectancy – is poverty. Yet migration – in part because it offers such opportunities on a global scale – seems to protect against the worst effects of poverty.

Of course, one response is to insist that we make *sure* that migrants do not ask *anything* of our welfare systems by creating systems that admit only wealthy migrants. This is, in many ways, what is happening right now. But this misses the point. If we care about fighting inequality, we need an immigration system that does not just set the rich free to move, but gives the poor equal opportunity to do so too.

10 MOVING FORWARD

In times of universal deceit telling the truth is a revolutionary act.
    Attributed to George Orwell

All the findings cited in this book show that there is very little evidence that immigration is responsible for any but a tiny percentage of income inequality, and ample evidence that immigration plays a vital role in propping up our public services and fuelling g economic growth. Yet immigration *policies* – fuelled by public fear – *are* exacerbating inequality, by creating a world in which freedom of movement is increasingly a privilege that only the rich can afford. The migration industry profits handsomely from the migration market: but borders do not bring social justice

When it comes to domestic inequality, immigration is a familiar bogeyman. Why would any state choose to admit *more* poor people? It's the low-skilled and low-paid who have to compete with migrant workers in the labour market. The poor here need protecting: surely that's our first duty. But this approach ignores the role migration can play as an escape route from poverty. For the 'huddled masses', migration *is* opportunity. Migration means birthplace need not be destiny. Whether measured in the $436 billion sent as remittances back by migrants from developing countries every year, the fifteen-fold average increase in income a migrant moving from Africa to North America enjoys, or the 50% of your wealth that was determined by the citizenship you acquired at birth, the connections between freedom of movement, social mobility and global equality are clear.

This is a short book. It doesn't answer many important questions about immigration: questions about culture and race, demography and language, integration and housing. But while it's important to recognise that immigration is not just about inequality – and that migration is never easy or unproblematic – the effect of immigration laws upon inequality cannot be ignored. If we care about combating entrenched privileges, the solution is not less migration, but more freedom of moment.

This doesn't mean calling for open borders: right now, open borders are political fantasy. There are also compelling reasons why – because of the inequalities that continue to persist within our own national communities – placing some conditions on migration right now is reasonable. But calling for a more open immigration policy should not be stigmatised as radical politics. As Jonathan Portes, Director of the National Institute for Economic and Social Research and an advocate for more liberal migration policies has remarked, 'I'm not saying something new … immigration might be one of the most controversial political issues today, but it's among the least controversial among economists'.[222] There is already a wealth of evidence showing the benefits that migration can bring, and which dispels the myths peddled by migration detractors. This makes it all the more galling that the migration policies being adopted today in countries such as the UK ignore the evidence. While such policies may appeal to popular sentiment, they will do nothing to challenge the fundamental structures that really perpetuate inequality, at home *and* abroad.

Yet with just a little imagination, it is possible to imagine an alternative set of progressive migration policies that could help to establish a more equal society.

One obvious place to begin is with policies that open up high-skilled migration. As we saw in Chapter 8, the very well-educated and the very well-paid are already partially exempt from having to fill quotas and pass resident labour market tests in the UK. Extending this to allow all-comers to apply for all graduate-level jobs would further a commitment to meritocracy, without risking the livelihoods of the poor. Local cohorts would still have built-in advantages: they are able not only to speak the language fluently, but to read more subtle cultural cues. Since the politics of migration makes talk of expanding migrants' rights so controversial, as an interim measure all students at UK universities should be able, upon graduating from a BA or B.Sc. degree, to apply for a two-year post-study visa and seek work. This half-measure isn't even innovative – it's simply returning to a system that used to exist in the UK until 2012.[223]

In fact, if we want to consider what an open, demand-driven labour market might look like, we could do worse that look to Sweden. Until 2008, Swedish labour migration was among the most restrictive system in the developed world: trade unions 'had, and used, an informal veto on recruitment'.[224] Today, its labour migration system is one of the most liberal. Employers – having first advertised the job to the local EU market for 10 days – can effectively recruit any worker, for any job, from anywhere, providing that the conditions of work are no lower than those agreed by trade unions in collective bargaining with employers.[225]

In the first three years of the programme, numbers of labour migrants grew steadily, as employers used to it to fill vacancies in both high- and low-skill 'shortage' occupations, from IT to berry-picking. Swedish workers working for firms recruiting labour migrants earn on average 10.5% more than those working in firms that don't. The result is that today, 'Sweden is the only OECD country where vacancies in low-skill occupations can be reliably and quickly be filled with workers recruited from abroad'.[226]

A second set of policies could focus on the other end of the labour market: low-wage, low-skilled but vital work. Here, the answer is not to protect 'our' poor by building walls, but to protect *all* poor workers by building a proper floor to the labour market. This does not mean just legislating for a minimum wage and health and safety regulations; it means enforcing these standards. Rather than railing about EU freedom of movement, a more productive place to begin would be to support strong reform of the Posted Workers' Directive, ending companies' 'social dumping'. An obvious adjunct to this is that – particularly in non-EU Western states without a mobile low-skilled labour force – visa quotas for low-skilled workers should expand, so that irregular migrants are brought out of the shadow economy.

Turning to those who are not just poor but persecuted, a third set of policy changes could help to build a fairer and more humane asylum system. Allowing asylum seekers to apply once more for permits to work –

rather than trapping them in penury and then blaming them for dependency – would restore to these individuals basic dignity and reduce the charge on the public purse. Those who lose their asylum claim – but meanwhile have managed to find steady work that pays a decent wage – could be offered the chance to regularise their status as a migrant worker. Again, this is not revolutionary: Sweden already operates one such scheme.[227]

Fixing asylum, however, is not just about better treatment for those who arrive. It is also about recognising that developing states cope with most of the demographic burden. Simply paying to sustain far-away refugee camps for decades – places that should 'burn holes in the consciences of all those privileged to live in better conditions'[228] – is not a measure of responsibility, but proof of its abrogation. The UK – along with nearly every other EU country– should expand its refugee resettlement programmes beyond a few token hundred. One way of doing this – which might help to dampen public concern about 'floods' of refugees – would be to focus not only on rescuing the most vulnerable, but on creating paths for the more resilient – younger, healthier and better-educated refugees – to work and study as *migrants*. When their initial visas expired, they would then be eligible to apply – as migrant workers – for some kind of indefinite leave to remain.[229]

In a similar vein, the West's commitment to international development should recognise the valuable role that international migration can play in enriching developing countries, not just as a result of remittance transfers but the accumulation of human capital. One often-raised concern is that those who are best able to migrate from poor countries are the middle-classes and elites. Yet we have seen that the West is in desperate need of low-skilled agricultural workers, while there is an abundant supply of these in developing states. The UK's Seasonal Agricultural Worker Programme could be reborn as a development initiative, in which short-term visas are issued to workers from developing states as part of a controlled temporary migration programme. In the US, Michael Clemens has been advocating for the adoption of such a programme for victims of the Haitian earthquake for the last three years. New Zealand already explicitly understands its temporary agricultural workers' programme in these developmentalist terms.[230]

In fact, once you begin thinking about migration in positive terms it's relatively easy to imagine how making incremental changes to our migration systems could combat inequality, not by locking migrants out, but promoting progressive migration. We are not short of new ideas.

But we are afraid to let go of the old ones.

The truth is that, for every positive speech about what migration could mean and every accompanying set of moderate, realistic policy proposals, there's little chance of much changing in the near future. Fear of immigration has become a self-perpetuating 'truth'. The mainstream politics consensus that being pro-immigration is toxic – a form of electoral suicide – means that every discussion about migration reform is really a discussion about migration restriction. This should be no surprise: outsiders have always been easy targets in teetering democracies. The result is that most migration advocates spend their time fire-fighting: struggling against new restrictions, new prejudices, new intolerance.

Until this changes, there's little point in focusing energies on bold new policies. The most immediate battles that need to be fought are about *removing* onerous restrictions that penalise average workers. Perhaps the most obvious example of this in Britain is the urgent need to remove the requirement for UK citizens to earn more than £18,600 before they can sponsor their partner to live with them in their own country, a rule which effectively disbars half of adult citizens from being able to marry and live in the UK if they fall in love with a foreigner.

Yet you can't change policies until you change minds. This is where *you* come in. We need to change the conversation we're having about migration: to challenge biased reporting with facts. This book is a starting place. You may not agree with all my answers – so use the evidence as a starting point to come up with new ones. The first step to take is to counter tabloid headlines and spurious assertions about what migrants 'do' to us with facts – whether that's over the dinner table, in the pub, or talking to the taxi driver on the way home. We *all* desperately need to hear both sides of the story: to remember that if we build a world where only the wealthy can migrate, average Britons will lose out too.

For talk to most successful second or third generation migrant families – whether their family arrived in Britain at the end of Empire from India, or whether their parents were ten-pound Poms who took a gamble fifty years ago and left England for Australia – and you'll usually find a migration story that has all the hallmarks of a rags-to-riches fairy-tale: migrants who arrived with nothing, but worked hard to make something and build a new, secure life for their children. There are, of course, stories of failure to balance those of success. But migration, until the 1970s, was a chance for the poor to re-roll Fortune's dice.

No longer. The freedom to move across international borders is increasingly dependent on first being lucky enough to either be born into a wealthy nation, and then having the personal wealth to negotiate the barriers designed to filter out the poor. A process of commodification – in which your right to move depends upon whether you can pay the price – is transforming international migration from one of the best weapons in the fight against inequality into a bureaucratic barrier impeding social mobility.

This should not surprise us. As leading Migration Studies academic Stephen Castles has observed, 'migration control is really about regulating North-South relationships and maintaining inequality. Only when the central objective shifts to one of reducing inequality will migration control become both successful and – eventually – superfluous'.[231]

The result is that today we live in a hyper-mobile world in which very few of us are entitled to, or can afford to, actually practice hyper-mobility. The migration debate is usually presented as a national problem: but we need to recognise it is also a class issue. This isn't just about the immigrants: it's about us, too. Ultimately, inequality – here, now – is too important to be sidelined, elided into a mean and petty conversation about immigrants' rights, while the rich convert legal freedom of movement into an elite privilege.

This is not a lost cause. Public opinion *can* change. Over time we have accepted – albeit slowly and often reluctantly – the rights of others that we were previously happy to deny: slaves, women, homosexuals. And ultimately, if you believe in progressive politics, you're an optimist. You have to believe in the possibility of change: that justice isn't just subjective, and that 'fair' isn't just self-interested. Certainly, when it comes to the politics of equality, there are many things to be angry about. But fearing and fighting immigration is a smokescreen. In the end, when it comes to progress, it is not the border guards who are standing on the right side of history.

It's the migrants.

ABOUT THE AUTHOR

Katy Long is a researcher and a writer whose works explores the causes and consequences of migration for migrants, citizens and communities. Katy is currently a Visiting Scholar at Stanford University and also teaches for the School of Advanced Study at the University of London.

Since completing her Ph.D. at the University of Cambridge in 2009, she has held faculty positions at the University of Oxford, the London School of Economics and the University of Edinburgh. Her first book, *The Point of No Return: Refugees, Rights and Repatriation* was published in 2013 by Oxford University Press and Katy is also the co-editor of *The Oxford Handbook of Refugee and Forced Migration Studies* (Oxford University Press, 2014).

Katy has also worked extensively with policy-makers including the United Nations High Commission for Refugees, the Norwegian Refugee Council and the Migration Policy Institute, as well as running the website migrantsandcitizens.org.

REFERENCES

[1] May, T., 'An immigration system that works in the national interest', 12 December 2012 https://www.gov.uk/government/speeches/home-secretary-speech-on-an-immigration-system-that-works-in-the-national-interest

[2] Obama, B., 'Remarks by the President on Economic Mobility', 4 December 2013, http://www.whitehouse.gov/the-press-office/2013/12/04/remarks-president-economic-mobility

[3] Oxfam, *Working for the Few: Political Capture and Economic Inequality*, Oxfam Briefing Paper No.178, 20 January 2014; Oxfam, *A Tale of Two Britains: Inequality in the UK*, 17 March 2014

[4] Piketty, T., (2014). *Capital in the Twenty-First Century*, Cambridge: Belknap Press

[5] BBC News, 'Cameron and Clegg under fire over foreign staff after "elite" claim', 7 March 2014, http://www.bbc.com/news/uk-politics-26481059

[6] Goodhart, D., (2013). *The British Dream: Success and Failure in Immigration Since the War*. London: Atlantic Books, p.xviii

[7] See e.g. Wright, O., 'Ukip election posters: Nigel Farage defends "racist" anti-immigration campaign ahead of Europe elections'; *The Independent*, 21 April 2014, http://www.independent.co.uk/news/uk/home-news/ukip-accused-of-scaremongering-in-antiimmigration-poster-campaign-ahead-of-european-elections-9273100.html; BBC News, 'Farage Has Momentum and is Targeting More Victories', 26 May 2014, http://www.bbc.com/news/uk-politics-27567744

[8] Mason, R., Watt, N. and Wintour, P., 'Cameron Panicking Over Romanian and Bulgarian Workers Says Labour'; *The Guardian*, 27 November 2013, http://tinyurl.com/ozsv4du

[9] Reid, S., 'A Year from now up to 29m Bulgarians and Romanians will have the right to settle in Britain and Claim Benefits', *The Daily Mail*, 23 December 2012; International Organisation for Migration, 'Press Release: World Migration Report 2011', 2 December 2011, http://www.iom.int/cms/en/sites/iom/home/news-and-views/news-releases/news-listing/lets-raise-migrants-voices-for-a.html#presskit

[10] Transatlantic Trends, *Immigration Survey: Topline Data*, Question 1a and D6 http://trends.gmfus.org/files/2011/12/TTI2011_Topline_final1.pdf

[11] Dominiczak, P., 'Labour Got it Wrong on Immigration, admits Miliband', *The Telegraph*, 14 January 2013, http://www.telegraph.co.uk/news/politics/9808290/Labour-got-it-wrong-on-immigration-admits-Miliband.html

[12] Office of the Prime Minister, 'Securing borders and reducing immigration: Immigration Speech by the Prime Minister', 25 March 2013, https://www.gov.uk/government/news/immigration-speech-by-the-prime-minister

[13] Goodhard, D., *The British Dream*, p. xxix.

[14] Stevenson, A., 'Dismay as Britain Accepts Just 50 Syrian Refugees', 27 June 2014, http://www.politics.co.uk/news/2014/06/27/dismay-as-britain-accepts-just-50-syrian-refugees

[15] 'German Jews Pouring into this Country', *Daily Mail*, 20 August 1938

[16] Lord Belpek, *House of Lords, Second Reading of the Aliens Act*, HL Deb 28 July 1905 vol 150 cc749-75

[17] Lazarus, E., 'The New Colossus', 1883

[18] see e.g. Joppke, Christian. 'Why liberal states accept unwanted immigration.' *World politics*, 50 (1998): pp.266–93.

[19] e.g. Collier, P., (2013). *Exodus: How Migration is Changing our World*. Oxford: Oxford University Press, p.5

[20] Collier, *Exodus*, p.5

[21] Finch, T, Andrew, H., and LaTorre, M., 'Global Brit: Making the Most of the British Diaspora', Institute for Public Policy Research, 2010; Office of National Statistics, *Migration Statistics Quarterly Report*, 27 February 2014, http://www.ons.gov.uk/ons/rel/migration1/migration-statistics-quarterly-report/february-2014/index.html

[22] Lalami, L., 'Immigration, a lexicon', 8 April 2013, https://twitter.com/LailaLalami/status/321285897746268161

[23] Transatlantic Trends, *Q28a*

[24] Transatlantic Trends, *Q28a*; Royal Statistical Society *Ipsos/Mori Perils of Perception: Topline Results*, 14–16 June 2013, Q12–13

[25] News 24, 'How Many Zimbabweans in SA?', 23 June 2009, http://m.news24.com/news24/SouthAfrica/News/How-many-Zimbabweans-in-SA-20090621; Polzer Ngwato, T., (2009). 'Zimbabwean migration to South Africa: from myth to management', *The Star Special Insert on Migration*, 6 December 2009, http://www.migration.org.za/publication/newspaper-article/2009/zimbabwean-migration-south-africa-myth-management-6-december-2009

[26] World Bank, *Migration and Development Brief*, April 2014, http://siteresources.worldbank.org/INTPROSPECTS/Resources/334934-1288990760745/MigrationandDevelopmentBrief22.pdf, p.2

[27] United Nations Development Programme, *Human Development Report 2009: Overcoming Barriers – Human Mobility and Development*, p.22, http://hdr.undp.org/en/media/HDR_2009_EN_Complete.pdf

[28] Wilhelm, K.E., 'Freedom of Movement at a Standstill? Towards the Establishment of a Fundamental Right to Intrastate Travel', *Boston University Law Review*, Vol. 90, 2010, pp.24-65 .

[29] UNDP, *Human Development Report* 2009, pp.22–24.

[30] ibid.

[31] *The Conservative Party Manifesto: Invitation to Join the Government of Britain,* 2010, p.21.

[32] Office of National Statistics, *Migration Statistics Quarterly Report,* 22 May 2014, http://www.ons.gov.uk/ons/rel/migration1/migration-statistics-quarterly-report/may-2014/index.html

[33] For critiques of the net migration policy see Glennie, A. and Cavanagh M., 'International Students and Net Migration in the UK', Institute for Public Policy Research, 14 May 2012; Mulley, S., 'Little progress towards immigration target comes at significant economic cost', Institute for Public Policy Research, 30 August 2012

[34] UN General Assembly, *Universal Declaration of Human Rights,* 10 December 1948, 217 A (III), Article 13.

[35]Milanovic, B., 'Global Income Inequality by the Numbers', *World Bank Policy Research Working Paper,* 6259, November 2012, http://elibrary.worldbank.org/docserver/download/6259.pdf?expires=1374262989&id=id&accname=guest&checksum=E87BEB0490CD5C8B812F9F8CE90948D2

[36] UNDP, *Human Development Report* 2009, p.24

[37] World Bank, *Migration and Development Brief,* April 2014 p.2.

[38] Rawls, J., (1971), *A Theory of Justice.* Cambridge: Belknap Press. Rawls' work did not consider migration, something that other academics repeatedly criticised. On the absence of migration in Rawls' work, see Benhabib, S. 'Borders, boundaries, and citizenship', *PS-WASHINGTON,* 38.4 (2005): p.673 and Rawls' later work, Rawls, J. (2001) *The law of peoples: with, The idea of public reason revisited.* Cambridge: Harvard University Press. Many scholars have used the *Theory of Justice* as a starting point for their own work on similar subjects including Sen, A., (2009). *The Idea of Justice,* Cambridge: Harvard University Press.

[39] Goodhart, *The British Dream,* p.xxv.

[40] Interview with M. Clemens, 6 June 2014.

[41] Bentham, J., A *Comment on the Commentaries* and *A Fragment on Government*. In Burns, J.H and Hart, H.L.A eds. (1977), *The Collected Works of Jeremy Bentham* p.393

[42]Sandel, M. J., 'The procedural republic and the unencumbered self.' *Political theory*, 12.1 (1984): pp.81–96.

[43] For more on nations as 'imagined communities' see Anderson, B. (1991, revised edition). *Imagined Communities: Reflections on the Origin and Spread of Nationalism*. London and New York: Verso

[44] Arendt, H., (1967, second edition.) *The Origins of Totalitarianism*. New York: Harvest, p.267.

[45] Domhoff, G.W., 'Wealth Income and Power: Who Rules America', *University of California at Santa Cruz*, *http://www2.ucsc.edu/whorulesamerica/power/wealth.html;* figures from the UK Wealth and Asset Survey 2008–2010, Office for National Statistics, including press release 3 December 2012, http://www.ons.gov.uk/ons/dcp171776_289407.pdf

[46] Goodhart, *The British Dream*, p.6.

[47] Most notably, see Walzer, M., (1983). *Spheres of Justice*, New York: Basic Books; Miller, D., (2012). *Global Justice and National Responsibility*. Oxford: Oxford University Press.

[48] European Commission, 'Schengen Area', http://ec.europa.eu/dgs/home-affairs/what-we-do/policies/borders-and-visas/schengen/index_en.htm

[49] Rutherford, A., 'Terrified Polish Family May Move Over Arson Attack', *The Belfast Telegraph*, 22 August 2012, http://www.belfasttelegraph.co.uk/news/local-national/northern-ireland/terrified-polish-family-may-move-over-arson-attack-28783752.html

[50] Hall, M., '79% say we must ban EU migrants', *The Express*, 30 January 2013, http://tinyurl.com/nh72ex7

[51] Benton and Petrovic, 'How Free is Free Movement?', p.3

[52] ibid. pp.3, 8–11

[53] 'Poles Earn Four Times As Much in UK, Pressure Group Claims', *The Telegraph*, 4 April 2012, http://www.telegraph.co.uk/news/uknews/immigration/9184207/Poles-earn-four-times-as-much-in-UK-pressure-group-claims.html; 'Average paid employment and average gross wages and salaries in enterprise sector in April 2014', http://inf.stat.gov.pl/gus/5840_1786_ENG_HTML.htm; Office of National Statistics, Annual Survey of Hours and Earnings, Provisional Results 2013, December 2013, p.36, http://www.ons.gov.uk/ons/dcp171778_335027.pdf

[54] See World Bank, *Bilateral Remittance Estimates 2012*, available from http://tinyurl.com/nttsqvq

[55] Finch et al, *Global Brit*, p.29

[56] Rigby, E., 'EU Migrants moving to UK balanced by Britons living abroad', *Financial Times*, 10 April 2014

[57] Kennedy, S., 'Measures to Limit Migrants' Access to Benefits', *House of Commons Library*, 15 May 2014, SN/SP/6889, p.14; 'Germany Moves to Expel Jobless Immigrants from other EU countries', *Rt.com*, 27 March 2014, http://rt.com/news/germany-expell-eu-immigrants-605/

[58] The A8 countries are Czech Republic, Hungary, Estonia, Latvia, Lithuania, Poland, Slovakia and Slovenia.

[59] Dustmann, C., Frattini, T., and Halls, C., 'Assessing the Fiscal Costs and Benefits of A8 Migration to the UK', *Centre for Research and Analysis of Migration Discussion Paper*, July 2009, http://www.cream-migration.org/publ_uploads/CDP_18_09.pdf

[60] Department of Work and Pensions, *Nationality at Point of National Insurance Number Registration of DWP Benefit Claimants: February 2011 Working Age Benefits*, January 2012, http://tinyurl.com/mjqwn2a

[61] 'France Moves Ahead on Posted Workers Without Waiting for Europe', EUACTIV.com, 14 January 2014, http://www.euractiv.com/trade/france-plays-solo-low-cost-worke-news-532718

[62] Novitz, T., 'UK Implementation of the Posted Workers Directive, 96/71', *Formula Working Paper*, No.12, 2010, http://www.jus.uio.no/ifp/english/research/projects/freemo v/publications/papers/2010/march/Formula-Novitz-2010.pdf

[63] Nielsen, N., 'Member States Agree Reforms on Foreign Workers Rules', *EU Observer*, 10 December 2013, http://euobserver.com/social/122409

[64] Tudor, O., 'MEPs should call halt to shoddy compromise on posted workers', 14 March 2014, http://touchstoneblog.org.uk/2014/03/meps-should-call-halt-to-a-shoddy-compromise-on-posted-workers/; Trades Union Congress (TUC), *Posted Workers' Directive Briefing for MEPs*, March 2014

[65] TUC, *Posted Workers Directive Briefing*; Nielsen, 'Member States Agree Reforms'

[66] Bigo, D., 'Immigration Controls and Free Movement in Europe', *International Review of the Red Cross*, Vol. 91, No.875, September 2009, http://www.icrc.org/eng/assets/files/other/irrc-875-bigo.pdf; Geddes, A., 'Getting the Best of Both Worlds? Britain, the EU and Migration Policy', *International Affairs*, 81:4, July 2005

[67] Frontex, 'Mission and Tasks', http://frontex.europa.eu/about-frontex/mission-and-tasks

[68] See e.g. Amnesty International, *Frontier Europe: Human Rights Abuses on Greece's Borders with Turkey*, 2013, 25/008/2013, http://tinyurl.com/kqhesr2

[69] Moloney, L., 'Italian Navy Rescues Hundreds of Migrants', *Wall Street Journal*, 12 June 2014, http://online.wsj.com/articles/italian-navy-rescues-hundreds-of-migrants-1402574649

[70] Haas, H., *Lampedusa: Only the Dead Can Stay*, 8 October 2013, http://heindehaas.blogspot.com/2013/10/lampedusa-only-dead-can-stay.html

[71] Malnick, E., 'Government Report Proposes 75,000 EU Immigration Cap', *The Telegraph*, 14 December 2013, http://tinyurl.com/mgbuw8t

[72] John Trickett MP, *House of Commons Debate*, 28 January 2008, col. 76, http://www.publications.parliament.uk/pa/cm200708/cmhansrd/cm080128/debtext/80128-0013.htm

[73]Ewalt, D.M., 'Immigration Reform Bill Is A Multi-Billion Dollar Bonanza For Defense Contractors', *Forbes Magazine*, 1 July 2013, http://www.forbes.com/sites/davidewalt/2013/07/01/immigration-reform-bill-is-a-bonanza-for-defensecontractors/

[74] Tarnapolsky, N., 'Israel built a new border wall to prevent migrants from 'Smuggling in Terror'', *Global Post*, 5 December 2013, http://www.globalpost.com/dispatch/news/regions/middle-east/131204/israel-new-border-wall-egypt-terrorism-immigration-project-hourglass

[75] Nesher, T., 'Netanyahu: Israel could be overrun by African infiltrators', *Haaretz*, 21 May 2012, http://www.haaretz.com/misc/iphone-article/netanyahu-israel-could-be-overrun-by-african-infiltrators-1.431589

[76] G4S, *What We Do: Immigration and Borders*' http://tinyurl.com/l7ovfv5; see also Corporate Watch, 'New Immigration Prison to Open at Gatwick this Spring', 29 January 2009, http://tinyurl.com/nvy2544

[77] Serco, *'About Us: Immigration Control'*, http://www.serco.com/markets/homeaffairs/immigration/index.asp; Townsend, M., 'Serco, the Observer, and a hunt for the Truth about Yarl's Wood Detention Centre', *The Observer*, 17 May 2014, http://tinyurl.com/n56p78s

[78] Tascor, *'What We Do: Immigration and Border Control'*, http://www.tascor.co.uk/what-we-do/immigration-and-border/; Lewis, P. and Taylor, M., 'G4S Security Company

Loses Bid to Renew Deportee Contract', *The Guardian*, 29 October 2010, http://tinyurl.com/k2spc78

[79] Bernstein, N., 'Companies Use Immigration Crackdown to Turn a Profit', *New York Times*, 28 September 2011, http://www.nytimes.com/2011/09/29/world/asia/getting-tough-on-immigrants-to-turn-a-profit.html?pagewanted=all&_r=0

[80] Bernstein, 'Companies Use Immigration Crackdown'; Greene J., Patel S., Briefing Materials Submitted to the United Nations Special Rapporteur on the Human Rights of Migrants. Washington, DC: Lutheran Immigration and Refugee Service and Detention Watch Network; 2007. 'The Immigrant Gold Rush: The Profit Motive Behind Immigrant Detention', in Detention and Deportation Working Group (ed.); pp.44–51

[81] Edwards, A., 'Measures of First Resort: Alternatives to Detention in Comparative Perspective', *Equal Rights Review*, Vol. 7, 2011: pp.117–42

[82] Home Affairs Select Committee, *Asylum: Seventh Report of Session 2013–2014*, 8 October 2013. Evidence of Stephen Small and Jeremy Stafford, 25 June 2013, Ev.32, Q.232 http://www.publications.parliament.uk/pa/cm201314/cmselect/cmhaff/71/71.pdf

[83] Home Affairs Committee Inquiry into Asylum, *Evidence from the Joseph Rowntree Foundation and the Housing and Migration Network, Submission by the Joseph Rowntree Foundation*, April 2013, p.7

[84] Home Affairs Select Committee, *Asylum: Seventh Report of Session 2013-2014*, 8 October 2013. Evidence of Stephen Small and Jeremy Stafford, 25 June 2013, Ev.32, Q.220

[85] Home Affairs Select Committee, *Asylum: Seventh Report of Session 2013–2014*, 8 October 2013, para. 92

[86] Farrell, P., 'Witnesses tell of Harrowing Conditions at Manus Detention Centre', *The Guardian*, 13 June 2014, http://www.theguardian.com/world/2014/jun/13/harrowing-

words-tell-of-cruel-degrading-conditions-at-manus-island; 'G4S Staff 'likely involved' in Manus riots', *NineNews*, 10 June 2014, http://news.ninemsn.com.au/national/2014/06/10/02/05/manus-island-inquiry-starts-with-g4s

[87] Hodges, J., 'G4S escapes Prosecution over 2010 Death as UK Charges 3 Guards, *Bloomberg.com*, 20 March 2014, *http://www.bloomberg.com/news/2014-03-20/g4s-escapes-prosecution-over-2010-death-as-u-k-charges-3-guards.html*; Corporate Watch, *G4S: Immigration,* http://www.corporatewatch.org/company-profiles/g4s-immigration

[88] Black, I., 'David Cameron: UK Arms Sales to Gulf "Legitimate"', *The Guardian*, 5 November 2012, http://www.theguardian.com/politics/2012/nov/05/david-cameron-arms-sales-gulf

[89] Allsopp, J., 'Sun, Sand… and Infinite Detention', *Open Democracy,* 3 March 2014, http://www.opendemocracy.net/5050/jennifer-allsopp/sun-sandand-indefinite-detention; author conversations March-April 2014

[90] See UNITE, *G4S – an issue for all trade unionists: G4S human rights briefing 11-18540,* 2013, http://tinyurl.com/knnpkwn

[91] Belsen, P., de Cock, M. and Mehran, F., 'ILO Minimum Estimate of Forced Labour in the World', ILO April 2005, http://tinyurl.com/75s2chl; World Bank Group, 'Human trafficking: a Brief Overview', 2009, http://tinyurl.com/3t9ykfz

[92] UNODC, 2010. *The Globalisation of Crime: A Transnational Organized Crime Threat Assessment*, p.39

[93] See Chapter 6 for more discussion of the costs associated with legal migration.

[94] ibid. p.56

[95] UNODC, 'Transnational Organised Crime: Smuggling of Migrants: The Search for a Better Life', http://www.unodc.org/documents/toc/factsheets/TOC12_fs_migrantsmuggling_EN_HIRES.pdf

[96] Human Rights Watch, *Hidden Emergency: Migrant Deaths in the Mediterranean*, 16 August 2012, http://www.hrw.org/node/109445; Anderson, S., 'How Many More Deaths? The Moral Case for a Temporary Worker Program?', *National Foundation for American Policy*, March 2013

[97] *Migration and Development Brief*, World Bank, 19 April 2013, http://tinyurl.com/pfc5a4l

[98] Altai Consulting, *ILO-UNHCR Cooperation Towards comprehensive Solutions for Afghan Displacement, Research Study on Afghan Deportees from Iran*, August 2008, http://www.unhcr.org/49ba32772.pdf, pp.28, 40

[99] The information about the Ugandan and Great Lakes passport markets in this chapter was gathered during fieldwork I carried out between July and September 2012 in Uganda.

[100] Names have been changed

[101] Henley and Partners, 'Citizenship of Choice', https://www.henleyglobal.com/citizenship/citizenship-planning/

[102] Henley and Partners, 'Why you need alternative citizenship', https://www.henleyglobal.com/citizenship/why-alternative-citizenship/

[103] Henley and Partners, *Visa Restriction Index: Global Ranking 2013*, http://tinyurl.com/q37hyyf

[104] ibid.

[105] UKBA, *Fees for Visa Applicants*, http://tinyurl.com/l3sbt46; UKBA, *Fees leaflet with effect from 6 April 2013*, http://tinyurl.com/c8rpbpb

[106] Emanuel, R. and Gutierrez, L., 'Priced out of Citizenship', *International Herald Tribune*, 3 April 2013, http://tinyurl.com/d5ycg3t; Sumption, M. and Flamm, S., 'The Economic Value of Citizenship for Immigrants in the United States', *Migration Policy Institute*, September 2012

[107] For details of application process see 'The St. Kitts & Nevis citizenship by investment programme', http://www.ciu.gov.kn/

108 See 'Dominica Economic Citizenship', http://www.invest-dominica.com/; 'Antigua and Barbuda Economic Citizenship', http://www.antiguacitizenship.com/; 'Granada Economic Citizenship', http://grenadaeconomiccitizenship.com/
109 Country Poverty Assessment, St Kitts and Nevis, 2007–8, Caribbean Development Bank, 4 August 2009, http://www.caribank.org/uploads/publications-reports/economics-statistics/country-poverty-assessment-reports/St.Kitts+and+Nevis+CPA+-+Vol.+1+Final+Report.pdf
110 For UK, see information at UKBA 'High Value Migrants', http://www.ukba.homeoffice.gov.uk/visas-immigration/working/tier1/; for US, 'EB-5 Immigrant Investor', http://tinyurl.com/mcnpzq6
111 Migration Advisory Committee, *Tier 1 Investor Route, Investment Thresholds and Economic Benefits,* February 2014, https://www.gov.uk/government/uploads/system/uploads/attachment_data/file/285220/Tier1investmentRoute.pdf
112 For summary of existing EU Property purchase/permanent residency schemes, see Shengan, Z., 'European Property Rules Aimed at Investors', *ChinaDaily.com.cn,* 3 December 2012, http://www.scmp.com/news/world/article/1145467/chinese-buy-property-cyprus-gain-eu-permanent-residence; also 'Residency for non-EU buyers of €500K homes', *The Local.es,* 21 May 2013, http://www.thelocal.es/20130521/rich-non-eu-housebuyers-tempted-by-500k-residency-deal
113 Warren, H., and Fontanella-Khan, J., 'Malta to Defy MEPs and Sell Citizenship for €650000', *The Financial Times,* 16 January 2014, http://www.ft.com/intl/cms/s/0/c68398a8-7ed9-11e3-a2a7-00144feabdc0.html#axzz34vIs4Z3B
114For details of regulations, see 'Family of Settled Persons', *UKBA, http://www.ukba.homeoffice.gov.uk/visas-immigration/partners-families/citizens-settled/spouse-cp/can-you-apply/*
115 Interview with D. Shillinglaw, September 2013.
116 Evidence from the *APPG Report on Family Migration*

[117] 'Middlesex University briefing: The fiscal implications of new Family Migration Rules: What does the evidence tell us?' 9 July 2013,
http://www.migrantsrights.org.uk/files/news/Family_migration_costs_briefing-9-7-2013.pdf
[118] US Citizenship and Immigration Services, *'Green Card through the Diversity Visa Immigrant Program'*,
http://www.uscis.gov/green-card/other-ways-get-green-card/green-card-through-diversity-immigration-visa-program/green-card-through-diversity-immigrant-visa-program
[119] Abadi, M.K., 'Venezuelans biggest winners of 2015 US Green Card Lottery', DV-2015, *Air Herald*, 5 June 2014,
http://airherald.com/venezuelans-are-biggest-winners-of-2015-us-green-card-lottery-dv-2015/1749/
[120] Law, A. O., 'The Diversity Visa Lottery: A Cycle of Unintended Consequences in United States Immigration Policy', *Journal of American Ethnic History*, Vol. 21, No. 4 (Summer, 2002), pp. 3-29: p.21
[121] see e.g. Baba, H., 'African Immigrants Worry about the Elimination of Diversity Visa', 8 May 2014,
http://kalw.org/post/african-immigrants-worry-elimination-diversity-visa. Because immigration reform efforts stalled in Congress in late 2013, the Border Security, Economic Opportunity and Immigration Modernization Act – which would have abolished the Diversity Lottery – did not pass into law.
[122] A refugee is someone who has a 'well-founded-fear of persecution for reasons of race, religion, nationality, membership of a particular social group or political opinion', UN General Assembly, *Convention Relating to the Status of Refugees*, 28 July 1951, United Nations, Treaty Series, vol.189, p.137, Art 1a
[123] UNHCR, 2014. *Global Trends 2013: War's Human Cost.* UNHCR Geneva, http://www.unhcr.org/5399a14f9.html

[124] 'Tories will be Tough on Bogus Asylum-Seekers', *The Daily Mail*, 5 November 2011 http://www.dailymail.co.uk/news/article-49963/Tories-tough-bogus-asylum-seekers.html

[125] See UKIP, *Statement of Principles: Immigration*, http://walsall.ukip.org/issues/policy-pages/immigration; Press Association, 'Nigel Farage calls on Government to let Syrian Refugees into UK', 29 December 2013, http://www.theguardian.com/politics/2013/dec/29/nigel-farage-syrian-refugees-uk

126 Tibbets G., 'Phil Woolas accuses asylum seeker lawyers and charities of "playing the system"', *The Daily Telegraph* 18 Nov. 2008, http://tinyurl.com/pakm9gx

[127] 'Asylum Seekers Arriving in Australia by Boat to be Resettled in Papua New Guinea', *ABC News*, 20 July 2013, http://www.abc.net.au/news/2013-07-19/manus-island-detention-centre-to-be-expanded-under-rudd27s-asy/4830778; MacKay, F., Thomas, S. and Kneebone, S., '"It Would be Okay If They Came through the Proper Channels": Community Perceptions and Attitudes toward Asylum Seekers in Australia', *Journal of Refugee Studies,* 2012)25 (1): pp.113–33

[128] Nick Clegg in Wintour, P., 'UK Agrees to Take 500 of the Most Traumatised Syrian Refugees', *The Guardian,* 29 January 2014, http://www.theguardian.com/world/2014/jan/28/syria-refugees-uk-agrees-up-to-500

[129] UNHCR, 2013. *Global Trends 2012: Displacement the New 21st Century Challenge,* UNHCR Geneva, p.3

[130] Paris, M., '"Bogus" asylum-seekers are not the problem; it's the millions of genuine refugees we should worry about', *The Spectator,* 7 December 2002, http://tinyurl.com/q7hmbyz

[131] Red Cross/ICM Poll and Press release, 'Public Massively Overestimate numbers seeking refuge in UK, British Red Cross Survey Finds', 8 June 2009

[132] UNHCR, *Global Trends* 2013

[133] UNHCR *Global Trends* 2012, p.3, Annexe Table 1 70–3; World Bank, *GDP Per Capita PPP (current international $)*, http://data.worldbank.org/indicator/NY.GDP.PCAP.PP.CD

[134] Gibney, M. J. and Hansen, R., *Asylum policy in the West: Past trends, future possibilities*. No. 2003/68. WIDER Discussion Papers//World Institute for Development Economics (UNU-WIDER), 2003

[135] Keung, N., 'Roma Refugees: Canadian billboards in Hungary Warn of Deportation', *The Star*, 25 January 2013, http://tinyurl.com/aeb55eg

[136] Barlow, K., 'Parliament Excises Mainland from Migration Zone', ABC News, 17 May 2013, http://www.abc.net.au/news/2013-05-16/parliament-excises-mainland-from-migration-zone/4693940

[137] 'Full Text: Tony Blair's Speech on Asylum and Immigration', *The Guardian*, 22 April 2005, http://www.theguardian.com/politics/2005/apr/22/election2005.immigrationandpublicservices

[138] Bitonti, D., 'Refugee Claims Down, as Ottawa hails reforms "tremendous success"', CTV News, 23 January 2014, http://www.ctvnews.ca/canada/refugee-claims-down-as-ottawa-hails-reforms-as-tremendous-success-1.1652294

[139] Home Affairs Select Committee, *Asylum: Seventh Report of Session 2013–2014*, 8 October 2013, written evidence submitted by the Amnesty International and the Still Human Still Here coalition (ASY 40), para.3

[140] Interview with D. Kayembe, May 2014

[141] ibid.

[142] Keith Vaz, Chair Home Affairs Select Committee in 'Asylum system under strain', 11 October 2013, http://tinyurl.com/lo7ccue

[143] Home Affairs Select Committee, *Asylum: Seventh Report of Session 2013-2014*, 8 October 2013, p.10, http://www.publications.parliament.uk/pa/cm201314/cmselect/cmhaff/71/71.pdf

[144] In April 2014, the High Court found that the UK Home Secretary's decision to freeze asylum support rates was 'flawed': see 2014 EWHC 1033, Case No: CO/8523/2013. See also: Ghelani, S., Government in the Dock: Destitution and Asylum in the UK, *Open Democracy*, 3 February 2014, http://www.opendemocracy.net/5050/sonal-ghelani/government-in-dock-destitution-and-asylum-in-uk
[145] Allsopp, J., Sigona, N. and Phillimore, J., *Poverty among Refugees and Asylum Seekers in the UK: An Evidence and Policy Review*, IRIS Working Paper Series No.1, 2014 http://www.birmingham.ac.uk/Documents/college-social-sciences/social-policy/iris/2014/working-paper-series/IRiS-WP-1-2014.pdf
[146] Home Office, *Asylum Policy Instruction: Permission to Work*, 1 April 2014, https://www.gov.uk/government/uploads/system/uploads/attachment_data/file/299415/Permission_to_Work_Asy_v6_0.pdf
[147] Taylor, D. and Townsend, M., 'Congolese Asylum Seekers Face 'Torture with Discretion' after Removal from UK', *The Observer*, 15 February 2014.
[148] Crawley, H., Hemmings, J. and Price, N., *Coping with Destitution: Still Human, Still Here*, Centre for Migration Policy Research, Swansea University, February 2011, http://stillhumanstillhere.files.wordpress.com/2009/01/oxfam_coping_with_destitution.pdf
[149] Office of National Statistics, *Immigration Statistics, January – March 2013*, 23 May 2013, http://tinyurl.com/q2f8dww
[150] Home Affairs Select Committee, *Asylum: Seventh Report of Session 2013–2014*, 8 October 2013, written evidence submitted by the British Red Cross (ASY 72)
[151] Wintour, 'UK Agrees to Take 500 Syrian Refugees'
[152] Fieldwork, Uganda, July–September 2012; OIOS, *Investigation Into Allegations Of Refugee Smuggling At The Nairobi Branch Office Of The Office Of The United Nations High*

Commissioner For Refugees, U.N. Doc A/56/733, December 21, 2001

[153] See e.g. Mitchell G. D., 'The Impact of U.S. Immigration Policy on the Economic "Quality" of German and Austrian Immigrants in the 1930s'. International Migration Review 1982; 26(3): pp.940–67.

[154] Hansard, House of Commons Debate (1933) United Kingdom. Hansard Parliamentary Debates, vol. 345. cc.3043–87.

[155] See e.g. the story of the *St. Louis* steamship, denied entry to Cuba, the US and Canada in 1939 while carrying more than 900 German Jewish refugees. Ogilvie S. and Miller S., *Refuge Denied: The* St. Louis *Passengers and the Holocaust.* Madison: University of Wisconsin Press; 2006, p.174

[156] House of Lords, Select Committee on Economic Affairs, *The Economic Impact of Immigration,* Vol. 1: Report, April 2008, p.22, http://tinyurl.com/254ug6

[157] ibid.

[158] Migration Advisory Committee, *Analysis of the Impacts of Migration,* January 2012, http://tinyurl.com/ogp88g5; see also House of Lords, *Economic Impact of Immigration,* p.23

[159] Clemens, M., and Pritchett, L., 'Income per natural: Measuring development as if people mattered more than places', 5 February 2008, http://tinyurl.com/prwf8wr

[160] Office of National Statistics, *Labour Market Statistics, April 2014,* http://www.ons.gov.uk/ons/dcp171778_357545.pdf; Clancy, G., 'Employment of Foreign Workers in the United Kingdom 1997 to 2008', *Economic and Labour Market Review,* Vol. 2: No.7, July 2008

[161] Slack, J., 'Migration is Killing Off Jobs: 160,000 Britons have missed out on employment because work was taken by foreigners', *The Daily Mail,* 14 January 2012, http://www.dailymail.co.uk/news/article-2084667/UK-unemployment-23-fewer-Britons-jobs-100-migrants.html

[162] The Migration Observatory, *New Migrants, 'New' Jobs, Old Confusion*, 1 February 2012,
http://www.migrationobservatory.ox.ac.uk/commentary/new-migrants-new-jobs-old-confusion%E2%80%A6
[163] Tier 2, 'Resident Labour Market Test',
http://www.ed.ac.uk/schools-departments/human-resources/recruitment/eligibility-immigration/recruiters-guidance/points-based/tier2/labour-market
[164] Ferguson, A. in Taylor, L., 'Foreign-players quota will harm Premier League, warns Ferguson', *The Guardian*, 8 August 2008,
http://www.theguardian.com/football/2008/aug/08/premierleague.manchesterunited
[165] United States Citizenship and Immigration Services, *H-1B Fiscal Year (FB) 2015 Cap Season*, http://tinyurl.com/mzukfe5; *USCIS Reaches FY 2014, H1-B Cap*, 8 April 2013,
http://www.uscis.gov/news/uscis-reaches-fy-2014-h-1b-cap
[166] Wadhwa, V., Saxenian, A. and Siciliano, F.D., 'America's New Entrepreneurs: Then and Now', October 2012,
http://tinyurl.com/mpv4e3y
[167] Harkinson, J., 'How H1-B Visas are screwing Tech Workers', *Mother Jones*, 22 February 2013,
http://www.motherjones.com/politics/2013/02/silicon-valley-H-1B-visas-hurt-tech-workers
[168] Rothwell, J. and Ruiz, N., *H1-B Visas and the STEM shortage*, 10 May 2013,
http://www.brookings.edu/research/papers/2013/05/10-H-1B-visas-stem-rothwell-ruiz
[169] OECD, *Recruiting Immigrant Workers: Sweden*, p.70,
http://browse.oecdbookshop.org/oecd/pdfs/product/8111191e.pdf
[170] See e.g. Ruhs, M. and Vargas-Silva, C., 'The labour market effects of immigration', *The Migration Observatory*, 5 March 2014,
http://www.migrationobservatory.ox.ac.uk/briefings/labour-market-effects-immigration; Dustmann, C., Glitz, A. and Frattini, T., 'The Labour Market Impact of Immigration.'

Oxford Review of Economic Policy 24, no. 3 (2008); Lucchino, P., Rosazza-Bondibene, C. and Portes, J., 'Examining the Relationship between Immigration and Unemployment using National Insurance Number Registration Data.' NIESR Discussion Paper 386, National Institute of Economic and Social Research, London, 2012

[171] Migration Advisory Committee, *Analysis of the Impacts of Migration.* The discrepancy between the 23/100 and 1 in 13 figures results from the fact that the first figure refers to the impact of newly arrived migrants during recession, while the second is an overall figure

[172] Devlin, C., Bolt, O., Patel, D., Harding, D. and Hussain, I., 'Impacts of Migration on UK Native Employment: An Analytical Review of the Evidence, *Home Office Occasional Paper,* March 2014, p.44

[173] Migration Advisory Committee, *Analysis of the Impacts of Migration,* pp.59, 66–67

[174] ibid.

[175] Borjas, G. and Katz, L., 'The Evolution of the Mexican-Born Workforce in the United States, pp.37, 63, https://www.aeaweb.org/assa/2006/0108_1015_0302.pdf

[176] Card, D. *Immigration and inequality.* No. w14683. National Bureau of Economic Research, 2009, p.31

[177] 'Immigration Minister Resigns for Employing Illegal Immigrant', *The Guardian,* 8 February 2014; Bingham, J. and Prince, R., 'Attorney General Baroness Scotland fined £5,000 over illegal immigrant housekeeper', *The Telegraph,* 22 September 2009

[178] See e.g. Anderson, B., (2000) *Doing the Dirty Work? The Global Politics of Domestic Labour.* London: Zed Books; Avendaño, Ana, *Mobilizing Against Inequality: Unions, Immigrant Workers, and the Crisis of Capitalism.* Eds. Lee H. Adler, Maite Tapia and Lowell Turner. Cornell University Press, 2014

[179] Leaker, D., 'Economic Inactivity', *Economic and Labour Market Review,* Vol 3: No. 2, p.42

[180] Anderson, B. (2010) 'British jobs for British workers? Understanding demand for migrant labour in a recession', *Whitehead Journal of Diplomacy and International Relations*, 10(1), Spring/summer 2010

[181] Cowley, U. (2001). (2001) *The Men who Built Britain: A History of the Irish Navvy.* Dublin: Wolfhound Press

[182] Doward, J., 'Migrant Job Squeeze Alarms UK Fruit Farmers', *The Guardian*, 25 May 2013, http://www.theguardian.com/business/2013/may/25/migrant-jobs-fruit-farms-kent

[183] Migration Advisory Committee, *Migrant Seasonal Workers*, pp.62–3

[184] ibid. pp.147–51

[185] ibid. p.4

[186] Migration Advisory Committee, *Migrants in Low-Skilled Work: The growth of EU and non-EU labour in low-skilled jobs and its impact on the UK: Full Report*, July 2014, http://tinyurl.com/kf6w9f5

[187] Whitehead, T., 'More than three million migrants under Labour', *The Telegraph*, 22 February 2011, http://www.telegraph.co.uk/news/uknews/immigration/8339075/More-than-three-million-migrants-under-Labour.html

[188] Grove-White, R., 'Viral Migrant Bashing', 16 August 2012, http://www.migrantsrights.org.uk/blog/2012/08/viral-migrant-bashing

[189] See e.g. Bommes, M. and Geddes, A., eds. *Immigration and welfare: challenging the borders of the welfare state.* Vol. 1. Psychology Press, 2000

[190] Centre on Budget and Policy Priorities, *Policy Basics: Where do our Federal Tax Dollars Go?*, 31 March 2014, http://www.cbpp.org/cms/?fa=view&id=1258

[191] UK Visas and Immigration, *Guidance: Public Funds*, 17 February 2014, https://www.gov.uk/government/publications/public-funds--2/public-funds

[192] Although they will receive contribution-based job seekers' allowance if made redundant, provided they have paid sufficient National Insurance contributions.

[193] Broder, T. and Blaze, J., *Overview of Immigrant Eligibility for Federal Programs*, National Immigration Law Centre, October 2011

[194] European Commission, *A Fact-finding Analysis on the Member States' Social Security Systems of the entitlements of non-active intra-EU migrants to special non-contributory cash benefits and healthcare granted on the basis of residence*, 2013, http://tinyurl.com/nmqpxgm

[195] ibid. p.169

[196] ibid. p.173

[197] ibid. p.175

[198] Dustmann et al, *Assessing the Fiscal Costs and Benefits of A8 Migration*, p.18

[199] George, A., Meadows, P., Metcalf, H., Rolfe, H., *Impact of Migration on the Consumption of Education and Children's Services and the Consumption of Health Services, Social Care and Social Services*, National Institute of Economic and Social Research, December 2011, p.51, http://tinyurl.com/q59wywt

[200] 'The Abuse of Migrants: And Still They Come', *The Economist*, 19 April 2014, http://www.economist.com/news/international/21601029-balancing-interests-migrant-workers-and-countries-they-live-and-still-they

[201] Goss, S., Wade, A., Skirvin, J.P., Morris, M., Bye, K.M., Huston, D., *'Effects of Unauthorized Immigration on the Actuarial Status of the Social Security Trust Funds'*, Actuarial Note Number 151, April 2013, http://www.socialsecurity.gov/oact/NOTES/pdf_notes/note 151.pdf

[202] Hall, M., 'Now 600,000 Illegals Are Given National Insurance Numbers in Labour Blunder', *The Express*, 16 January 2008, http://tinyurl.com/ppcq5w9

[203] Foxton, W., 'Why Tories Ought to Hate the Immigrant Health Tax', *The New Statesman,* 4 July 2013, http://www.newstatesman.com/politics/2013/07/why-tories-ought-hate-immigrant-health-tax; Home Office, *Controlling Immigration: Regulating Migrant Access to Health Services in the UK,* 3 July 2013, p.17, http://tinyurl.com/pe4b565

[204] Prederi, 'Quantitative Assessment of Visitor and Migrant Use of the NHS in England', https://www.gov.uk/government/uploads/system/uploads/attachment_data/file/251909/Quantitative_Assessment_of_Visitor_and_Migrant_Use_of_the_NHS_in_England_-_Exploring_the_Data_-_FULL_REPORT.pdf

[205] ibid. pp.17-20

[206] Hanefeld, J., Horsfall, D., Lunt, N., Smith, R., (2013), 'Medical Tourism: A Cost or Benefit to the NHS?', PLoS ONE 8(10): e70406. doi:10.1371/journal.pone.0070406

[207] BBC News, *In Full – David Cameron's Immigration Speech,* 14 April 2011, http://www.bbc.com/news/uk-politics-13083781

[208] General Medical Council, *The State of Medical Education and Practice in the UK 2013,* p.22 *http://www.gmc-uk.org/SOMEP_2013_web.pdf_53703867.pdf*

[209] Australian Bureau of Statistics, 4102.0 – Australian Social Trends: Doctors and Nurses, 10 April 2013, http://www.abs.gov.au/ausstats/abs@.nsf/Lookup/4102.0Main+Features20April+2013

[210] Global Health Workforce Alliance and World Health Organisation, *A Universal Truth: No Health Without a Workforce,* November 2013, http://tinyurl.com/ptvwldf

[211] Wolf, J., 'Why America Steals Doctors from Poor Countries', *The Guardian*, 4 April 2011, http://www.theguardian.com/education/2011/apr/04/america-steals-doctors-from-developing-countries; Clemens, M., 'People are not property: Please stop saying that countries 'steal' doctors from Africa', 6 April 2011, http://tinyurl.com/3bnuguh

[212] Clemens, M. and McKenzie, D., 'Think Again: Brain Drain', *Foreign Policy,* 22 October 2009, http://www.foreignpolicy.com/articles/2009/10/22/think_again_brain_drain

[213] House of Commons Education Committee, *Underachievement in Education by White Working Class Children*, First Report of Session 2014–2015, 11 June 2014, p.16, http://www.publications.parliament.uk/pa/cm201415/cmselect/cmeduc/142/142.pdf

[214] Jimenez, T. and Horowitz, A., 'White Is Just Alright: How Immigrants Redefine Achievement and Reconfigure the Ethnoracial Hierarchy', *American Sociological Review,* 78(5), 2013, pp.849–71: 865, 859.

[215] George et al, *Impact of Migration,* 2011, p.25

[216] Bell, B., 'Immigration and Crime: Evidence from the UK and other Countries', *The Migration Observatory,* 13 November 2013

[217] Immigration Policy Centre, *From Anecdotes to Evidence: Setting the Record Straight on Immigration and Crime,* 25 July 2013, http://www.immigrationpolicy.org/just-facts/anecdotes-evidence-setting-record-straight-immigrants-and-crime-0

[218] Sampson, R. J. and Byron Groves, W., 'Community structure and crime: Testing social-disorganization theory'. *American journal of sociology* (1989): 774–802

[219] Bell, B. and Machin, S., 'Immigrant Enclaves and Crime', *CEP Discussion Paper No. 1104,* December 2011, http://cep.lse.ac.uk/pubs/download/dp1104.pdf

[220] Stowell, J.I, Messner, S.F., McGeever, K.F. and Raffalovich, L.E. (2009), 'Immigration and the recent violence crime drop in the United States: a pooled, cross-sectional time-series analysis of metropolitan areas'. *Criminology,* 47(3), pp. 889-928

[221] UN General Assembly, *Universal Declaration of Human Rights,* 10 December 1948, 217 A (III), Article 25 and 26, http://www.refworld.org/docid/3ae6b3712c.html

[222] Interview, J. Portes, May 2014

[223] 'UK Post-Work Study Visa: Updated January 2013', visited 27 June 2014, http://www.workpermit.com/uk/tier-1-visas-post-study-work.htm

[224] OECD, *Recruiting Immigrant Workers: Sweden*, p.11

[225] ibid. p.12, pp.56–66

[226] ibid. p. 67

[227] Swedish Government, 'Asylum seekers who have got a job and want to apply for a work permit, http://tinyurl.com/lnwcmpv

[228] Van Heuven Goedhart, J., United Nations High Commissioner for Refugees, *Nobel Prize Acceptance Speech*, 12 December 1955, http://www.nobelprize.org/nobel_prizes/peace/laureates/1954/refugees-lecture.html

[229] For more on this see Long, K., 'Extending protection?: labour migration and durable solutions for refugees', *New Issues in Refugee Research*, UNHCR Working Paper Series, *http://www.unhcr.org/4ad334a46.pdf* (2009)

[230] Interview with M. Clemens, June 2014; Gibson, J. and McKenzie, D., 'Development through Seasonal Worker Programs: The Case of New Zealand's RSE Program', CREAM working paper 05/14, 2014, http://www.cream-migration.org/publ_uploads/CDP_05_14.pdf

[231] Castles, Stephen. 'Why migration policies fail'. *Ethnic and Racial Studies* 27.2 (2004): pp. 205–27, 227

CPSIA information can be obtained at www.ICGtesting.com
Printed in the USA
LVOW06s0934050915

452965LV00027B/1176/P

9 781506 185415